Enough IS Enough

Shattering the Myth that
Women must have it all, do it all & be it all

By

Farah Brown & Sam Bramwell

© Copyright 2025 by Farah Brown & Sam Bramwell
All rights reserved.

This publication, including all text, images, and intellectual content, is protected under copyright law. Unauthorised reproduction, duplication, distribution, or transmission of this material, in any form, is strictly prohibited. Additionally, this content may not be used, in whole or in part, for the training, development, or enhancement of machine learning algorithms or artificial intelligence systems without the express written consent of the publisher.

Published by Femnesty
www.femnesty.com

PRINT ISBN 978-1-0684045-0-4

This book is dedicated to our mothers whose strength, wisdom, and love shaped us into the women we are today. It is also for our daughters and all future generations of women; may you inherit a world where balance, equality, and well-being are not just dreams but realities.

Contents

Introduction .... - 1 -

Part One: Unveiling The Myth 7

Chapter One: The Elusive Dream of 'Having it All' 9

Chapter Two: Invisible Work (a nod to Invisible Women) 21

Chapter Three: The Impact of the Myth 51

Part Two: Living the Myth 73

Chapter Four: The Weight of Guilt and Shame 75

Chapter Five: Building 89

Chapter Six: Balancing 107

Chapter Seven: Transitioning 135

Part Three: A New Dawn for Women in the 21st Century 165

Chapter Eight: Breaking the Silence 167

Chapter Nine: A Future Beyond the Myth 207

Acknowledgments 219

Bibliography 220

Endnotes 224

Enough is Enough

Introduction

In a world where relentless change collides with soaring expectations, the narrative of women's evolving roles and contributions in society, the workplace, and home is a stark testament to ambition, struggle, and the relentless pursuit of equality and balance.

Women, from high-profile executives to key roles across every sector, navigate a treacherous landscape of professional fulfillment fraught with systemic barriers. *The broken rung, the glass ceiling and the glass cliff, the gender pay gap, the wealth and health gaps, the 2nd shift, gender-based violence, the motherhood penalty*, and *gendered ageism*, are not just statistics; they are daily realities that sabotage women's progress and perpetuate inequality. This is more than a story of individual perseverance, it's a call to dismantle the entrenched injustices that hold women back, demanding urgent, transformative action.

Our stories highlight a journey and dilemma familiar to many women, one that is often unspoken or silenced. As working mothers and women in demanding roles, we find ourselves questioning the myth of 'having it all, doing it all, and being it all'. What is the true cost to our emotional, physical, and financial health?

At 42, amidst a tumultuous health crisis, Farah faced a major operation during a peak work season. With limited time for recovery, she returned to work two weeks post-surgery, immediately followed by extensive travel. 'I just had to keep going,' Farah reflects, capturing the struggle of her relentless pace. The surgery precipitated an early menopause, a profound and solitary challenge.

Fourteen months later, compounded by demanding work conditions, Farah reached a tipping point - a complete burnout, echoing years of unwavering effort, working through childbirth to undergoing a hysterectomy. 'It hit me like never before,' she confesses. Fortunate to have a support network, she recognises that many are not as privileged.

This narrative is a thread weaving through many of our lives; the constant race, the effort to catch our breath while career building, managing children's activities, and fulfilling the multiple roles we find ourselves pursuing. These responsibilities, coupled with the expectation of personal well-being, form an overwhelming tapestry. 'And let's not even delve into our Covid experiences; that's a story in itself, right?'

Sam's journey shows the challenges women face in navigating the complexities of modern life. Diagnosed with ovarian cancer at 27 and thrust into infertility and surgical menopause, she immersed herself in her career as a coping mechanism. The birth of her children, 10 years later, through egg donation

& IVF marked a new chapter, one filled with love but also new obstacles. Returning to work after the birth of her first child, Sam encountered gender inequalities as her role was unfairly replaced during her absence. Her story highlights the pressure women endure to balance professional aspirations with familial responsibilities, often at the cost of their own well-being.

Our collaboration comes at an opportune time, driven by a shared passion to bring to light the unique challenges faced by women in the 21st century. We recognise the freedoms our mothers and grandmothers fought for in marriage, society, and the workplace. Freedom continues to be elusive, and progress has slowed.

As we write this, we're aware of organisations slashing their Diversity, Equity, and Inclusion budgets and renouncing their programmes. We hope the stories shared in this book, empower leaders to reflect on these decisions and reverse them. Our conversations with women and leaders in researching this book suggests fatigue, budget cuts, and polarisation are part of the problem; yet, as we enter the age of Artificial Intelligence (AI), if women are not equally at the table developing AI strategies, we will be written out of the AI story and bias will continue to harm us.

We aspire to greatness in all aspects of our lives, and we have access to education, careers, and choice over our fertility. We're told we can 'have it all', but at what cost?

We aim to dismantle the myth of 'having it all', a myth that burdens women with endless juggling of work, personal life, self-neglect, the pressure to be a 'sex goddess', continual 'leaning in', always being a present parent and aspiring to top-tier professional success.

This myth has morphed into doing it all and being it all. This pursuit has far-reaching impacts, affecting health, careers, lives, partnerships, and society at large. **It's important to point out, we want women to have autonomy to define their version of success what 'having it all' means to them. But we must recognise that the system is broken, and it fails to support us in achieving our ambition.**

From the outset, our goal has always been to make visible the 'invisible' and share the unspoken, unheard stories of women to shine a light on the challenges and obstacles they faced. We hope by doing so, we can, once and for all, create social awareness and action.

Sharing stories is part of the evolutionary fabric of our societies, an often-lost tradition and a way to challenge dominant narratives that have sought to erase, ignore, oversimplify, and universalise the experiences of women. We know from holding space for professional women how empowering it is to locate ourselves within the stories of others and how often the opportunity is missed to enable that outcome.

Having ventured deep into the heart of this pervasive myth, through our survey, interviews and discussions with numerous women, it's evident this terrain is fraught with complex challenges. Our aspiration is not to undermine women's choice, nor define the boundaries of what is right or wrong for any woman. Rather, we aim to respect and understand the nuanced realities each woman faces. We hope to contribute to a dialogue that honours the strides made and amplifies strides still needed, furthering our collective journey towards equality, autonomy, and choice.

Our book is not about whether a woman should or should not have a career, become a parent, do both or neither. It focuses on the central issue faced by millions of women striving to do everything and, as our research shows, finding themselves trapped by unseen barriers and unachievable standards, burdens that often contribute to a second-class status in society and the workplace.

Women stand at the intersection of progress and tradition, grappling with career pressures, familial responsibilities, and societal expectations of beauty, fitness, and perfection. As we delve into these challenges, we will offer a nuanced view of the world's women navigate daily.

Enough is Enough begins to explore the often-overlooked challenges men face amidst evolving gender dynamics and changing roles. We see the impact of emotional repression and its impact on men's mental health & society. We believe the path to change is for women and men to support each other equally, fostering inclusive dialogue, acknowledging that a healthier work-life balance demands empathy, understanding, and active participation from all genders and a commitment to change on both sides. We invite our men to begin their emotional work, so we can walk this path together.

We will peel back the layers of systemic issues contributing to women's burnout and departure from their careers, through this we hope to remind you burnout is not a personal failure it's the logical outcome of a system that turned rest into a luxury and overwork and toxic achievement into a moral value. We explore strategies for individuals and organisations to foster sustainable, supportive environments. Our narrative is deeply personal and reflective of real-life experiences.

Enough is Enough is more than a book; it's a movement towards a more empathetic and inclusive society. As we turn these pages together, let's commit to learning, unlearning, and reimagining our roles in creating a world where balance is not just an aspiration but a reality.

Welcome to Enough is Enough – a journey towards understanding, change, inclusion and belonging.

Unveiling The Myth

Part One

Chapter One:
The Elusive Dream of 'Having it All'

In the maze of modern 21st Century life, the quest for women to 'have it all' has morphed into a complex narrative of ambition, sacrifice, and the incessant tug-of-war between fulfilling family lives, personal wellbeing, and professional achievement. 24/7 pressure from social media has raised the stakes of this dream, consistently shifting the boundaries of what it is to be a woman in these times. As we will explore, the myth, impacts us all, but for women it is especially challenging.

The term 'Having it All' gained fame in the 1980s, largely attributed to Helen Gurley Brown's book, *Having It All: Love, Success, Sex, Money*. This book painted a picture of women's empowerment predominantly through the lenses of appearance, money, diet, exercise, and sex. However, it sidestepped the real challenges of motherhood alongside a career. Similarly, Dame Shirley Conran's *Superwoman* (1975) encouraged women to embrace efficiency and reject perfectionism to manage the demands of modern life.

Whilst these books felt revolutionary at the time, they often overlooked the systemic barriers women faced and further placed the responsibility of 'achieving it all, doing it all, and being it all' firmly on women's shoulders.

Sam recalls growing up with Superwoman on her mum's bookshelf, believing it held the key to womanhood. 'Back then, it felt empowering,' she reflects. 'Yet, I witnessed my mum labour hard under the pressure of juggling her multiple roles as a single parent, full-time hospital sister and caregiver to her parents. Over time, it took a huge toll on her mentally and physically.'

As we dissect the myth, it becomes evident that the very foundation of this concept is built on unrealistic expectations. Almost 50 years later, women are burdened by almost constant gender and financial oppression. The narrative, often portrayed as a beacon of female empowerment, glosses over the inherent challenges and sacrifices involved to be a woman in the 21st Century, often forcing women into a scarcity mindset, perpetuating feelings of perfectionism, people-pleasing, inadequacy, fear and shame, despite our numerous achievements.

As the stories shared in this book show, even though we've made considerable progress toward gender equality, the path remains fraught with inequalities. Each story isn't just a narrative, it's a raw, unfiltered look at the intense, often invisible sacrifices women make to progress in the personal and professional lives. The accounts of these women coupled with extensive insights from a survey of over 370 women from various walks of life, illustrate the nuanced experiences women face every day. The impact of the nuclear family, globalisation, single parenthood, navigating special needs education, financial independence and a career, whilst at the same time being expected to be the primary carers, doers and thinkers in the home.

We've witnessed women in the public eye struggle. In 2023, Jacinda Ardern, New Zealand's prime minister, stepped down after nearly six years in office. Often viewed as a trailblazer, a new mother who breastfed in Parliament and steered her country through multiple crises, including the pandemic,

Ardern's decision to resign came as a surprise. As she put it, 'I know what this job takes, and I know that I no longer have enough in the tank to do it justice.' She also expressed her desire to spend more time with her family, stating: 'I am looking forward to spending time with my family again.'[i] Her frustration echoed the struggle of millions of women who consistently walk the line between balance and burnout.

As Amy Westervelt shares in her best-selling book *Forget Having It All*, 'We expect women to work like they don't have children and raise children as if they don't work.' The pressures of society have morphed compared to 60 years ago. Women are expected to look and act perfectly, plan every inch of their life, want to get married, not get married, build a career, know when exactly to have children, or choose not to have children and ultimately be punished for their choice.

Our survey elicited hundreds of differing interpretations of the 'myth of having it all'. Over 80% of the women who responded shared how it negatively impacted their lives, through pressure, guilt, shame, emotional labour and discrimination.

Indeed, it was through this commentary and our interviews we realised the myth of 'having it all' had somehow mutated into 'doing and being it all' over the past 40 years. Just as Senator Kirsten Gillibrand wrote in her book, *Off the Sidelines*,[ii] 'Let's stop talking about having it all and start talking about the real challenges of 'doing it all.' Our core dilemma remains how to balance the scales of a demanding career and a rewarding personal life without tipping over.

For some women this myth represents an unattainable goal of perfect balance across professional and personal spheres. A few respondents reflect on the term with nuance, suggesting that 'having it all' might vary from person to person, and what constitutes 'all' can be subjective and fluid. For others, it's a harmonious blend of career, family, and self, or recognising and appreciating what one has now, finding contentment in presence and fulfilment in the roles they prioritise. One respondent noted the liberation of having a job she finds fulfilling but not pursuing a career and finding freedom in that concept.

For the majority, the phrase meant oppression, where the responsibility for 'fixing' themselves under consumerist ideologies deepens the already cavernous gender pay and wealth gaps.

Ruth Rosen, a scholar who has written extensively about the history of feminism shared in a NY Times article,[iii] 'You can't find much archival evidence of the phrase before the tail end of the '70s - and even then, it wasn't so much a feminist mantra as a marketing pitch directed toward the well-healed liberated consumer.'

Neoliberalist feminism has us believe we can be empowered women, and success is ours for the taking; however, society, systems and gender roles haven't transformed enough to enable that ideal. Instead, we are very much playing dual roles: producer of offspring and producer of work, without adequate support.

Through Farah's journey, the harsh realities of striving to 'have it all' came to light. Her return to work merely two weeks postpartum, driven by a sense of duty and the fear of professional setback, spotlights the intense pressures working mothers face. The silent struggle with postpartum depression, the guilt of dividing time between work and family, and the juggle of responsibilities with a second child on the way paint a vivid picture of the toll this pursuit can take.

Her experiences echo the sentiment that behind every successful woman lies an untold story of sacrifices, unacknowledged struggles, the constant juggle between different roles. Farah's reality was even more brutal than it seemed. During the six-week check-up after the birth of her firstborn, she broke down in her GP's office, overwhelmed by the emotional anguish of balancing a newborn and a demanding job. Instead of empathy, she received a cold, dismissive response: 'Don't worry, I did the same. Whoever feeds your baby a bottle of milk will be their mummy, and they won't know the difference.' Those words, spoken with a smile, cut deep, intensifying her sense of guilt and inadequacy.

This exchange captures the broader societal expectations placed on women, to seamlessly navigate motherhood and career without complaint or visible struggle. Farah's emotional turmoil remained hidden, her tears shed in private, as she observed other working mothers who seemed to manage effortlessly. She believed she had to match their facade of perfection, internalising the notion that showing any weakness would undermine her professional standing.

Raised by a hardworking single mother, Sam was intimately acquainted with the precarious dance of managing a career, raising children, and staying afloat financially. Those formative years ignited a resolve in her to avoid the financial hardships her mother endured. Reflecting on her own path, Sam acknowledges the challenges: 'I've worked tirelessly for financial independence and security, but I'm ensnared in the constant mental load and, the silent expectation, that, because I'm a woman, I should inherently manage the household and take on the menial tasks at work.'

'It's the presumption that to "have it all" we must "do and be it all" that weighs heavily', Sam states. Her mind was engaged in perpetual planning, always sorting and aligning the various elements of work, school runs, meals, shopping, family celebrations, medical appointments, not to mention the barrage of her own health requirements and the relentless battle against workplace discrimination. She recalls the inappropriate intrusions by male colleagues, personal questions that were both unwarranted and uninvited, a vivid reminder of the extra burdens carried.

Sam recognises her most significant oversight was not seeking assistance and setting firm boundaries. 'I was too exhausted to initiate those crucial conversations', she admits, now realising the importance of establishing limits and communication. She further reflects: 'I was also too afraid to ask for help and feared being seen a failure or weak, especially at work, where I had to 'man up'. This retrospective insight shows the complexity of Sam's journey, one shared by many women who navigate these exhaustive responsibilities often without support.

The reality is stark - Women are being punished under outdated societal systems, working practises and fixed gender biases, driven to achieve more under the banner of 'having it all'. Traditional views on the roles of women versus men in relation to childcare and housework are creating a female health crisis, as the burden of childcare responsibility falls to women. 'Having it all' is weaponised against women daily as bias and discrimination leak out into the daily narrative and experiences of women.

Sadly, there are still not enough women in positions of power to make significant, systemic change for all women. Whilst board level appointments for women have increased in the UK and US (UK FTSE 350: *40% of board appointments are women*[iv]; US Russell 3000: *30% are women*[v]), only 10% of the FTSE 350 CEOs are women, this drops to 8.2% in the US, even lower for women of colour.

Worryingly, the average tenure of female CEO's is significantly shorter than that of their male counterparts. Women typically remain in role for just 5.2 years compared to 8.1 years for men.[vi] The challenge is further exacerbated by the declining growth rate of women in senior leadership, which fell to its lowest level in a decade in 2023, despite women making up approximately 70% of the workforce in many Western countries. The question we need to ask is why?

There are glimmers of progress, more girls are attending university than ever before and according to a 2024 Financial Times (FT) article,[vii] British young women in their 20's and 30's are beginning to out-earn their male peers in urban area. For the first time, women are more likely to be economically active than young men. This raises the hope that on merit and intelligence alone, more women will take up their positions of power alongside their male counterparts and make changes to the legacy structures that hold us back. However, the same article issues a warning: 'Who is doing most of the legwork raising children, who is out working to bring home a good income?' Increasingly, the answer is women.

The flip side to this progress is the growing disenfranchisement of young boys and men. As we seek greater inclusion for women, it must not come at the expense of men. True equality is about collaboration and parity, power with, not power over.

The challenge before us is not just about advancing one group over another, this approach hasn't worked. We must redefine how we coexist, work together, and reintegrate feminine and masculine principles to create a more balanced, compassionate and inclusive world, with systems that support us all. We must breakdown all the stereotypes of work inside and outside the home and encourage partnership across all aspects of life.

The reality is the myth of 'having it all' hurts men too. While women are expected to juggle career, care-giving and personal fulfilment seamlessly, men are conditioned to prioritise work above all else. Men who take on caregiving roles face stigma, perceived as 'helping out' rather than being equal partners.

With the rise of enhanced paternity leave, more men are experiencing the workplace penalties women have faced for decades. These ingrained pressures discourage men from fully participating in caregiving and domestic responsibilities, reinforcing legacy gender roles and slowing progress toward true equality.

The myth of 'having it all', isn't just a lie, it's a broken system that fails us all. Women don't lack ambition, skill or resilience and we don't believe men are the enemy. The real issue is a structure that expects women to carry the weight of work and home while pressuring men to prioritise career over care. we don't need more leaning in, we need workplaces, policies and cultures to acknowledge the importance of shared responsibility. Just as our grandmothers marched for freedom, we now fight for the rights of our daughters and our sons.

Enough is Enough. It's time to rewrite the rules together.

A Note to Male Allies
How do you feel about the myth of 'having it all' and who benefits from that belief? Take time to reflect on what you feel it means to you. How is this playing out in your work and home space? Do you observe any gender imbalances? How does this concept relate to you in your daily life? If you are a leader, what can you do to amplify female leaders in your organisation? Do you observe women being held to impossibly high standards?

Pause and Reflect

What areas of your life currently feel most out of balance, and how might redefining your personal idea of 'success' help you address this imbalance?

Think about the support networks in your life, professional and personal. What changes or additions would make these networks feel more meaningful and helpful to you?

Imagine speaking to someone struggling with the concept of 'having it all'. What would you share with them to encourage a healthier and more realistic perspective on balancing life and work?

'Each time a woman stands up for herself, without knowing it possibly, without claiming it, she stands up for all women'.
— *Maya Angelou*

Chapter Two
Invisible Work (a nod to Invisible Women)

In recent years, the terms 'Emotional Labour', 'Mental Load', and 'Second Shift' have emerged from the shadows of unrecognised women's toil into the mainstream conversation on gender inequality. These issues are increasingly acknowledged as a major hindrance to women's personal and professional progress, and our wellbeing.

These terms describe the invisible, continuous tasks that incessantly tug at the seams of women's attention, exhausting mental energy and time throughout our day and night.

Our survey revealed that even where women are the breadwinners or where there is a perceived division of labour, they still disproportionately bear the brunt of emotional labour and the mental load. A constant hum of over-responsibility and overwork: the barrier to 'having it all'.

At work, it is both the 'office housework tasks' associated with 'low promotability', [viii] such as planning a team offsite, ordering lunch, or leading the employee resource group.

These tasks run alongside our day jobs. Then it is the constant checking of our behaviour (the emotional labour), the expectation we must display empathy, take on the 'nurturing' role, or manage our emotions whilst portraying confidence, competence, but never show assertiveness (mistaken for aggression).

Unfortunately for women, this work has a negative impact, 'draining women's time and resources without equitable rewards, making it difficult for women to legitimise their power',[ix] and ultimately break the glass ceiling.

At home, the weight is even heavier. Women carry out the 'second shift', alongside more emotional labour. This second shift is an unpaid, relentless cycle of domestic and caregiving responsibilities that do not decrease as they advance professionally. Studies conducted last year show mothers reported being responsible for 73% of all cognitive labour, and 63% of all physical labour compared to their partners.[x] Further research shows senior women are over four times more likely to do more housework than their equivalent senior male counterpart.[xi]

So, it seems despite progress in gender equality, women still carry the overwhelming burden of childcare and domestic labour. In the UK, women provide 23.2 billion hours of unpaid childcare annually, valued at £382bn, compared to 9.7 billion hours by men (£160bn).[xii] Another study found women in heterosexual relationships take on far more cognitive and emotional labour than men.[xiii]

While only 9% of Britons now believe men should be sole breadwinners (down from 48% in the 1980s), 63% of women said they still do more than their fair share of housework and 32% of men admit they do less than they should. [xiv]

In the US, according to the US Bureau of Labor Statistics,[xv] mothers spend 2.7 hours per day on childcare as a primary activity, compared to 1.6 hours for fathers. For children under six, mothers average 7.5 hours of daily care, while fathers spend 5.3 hours.

Data from Pew Research Center reflects how the division of labour has changed over time, however while fathers have increased the amount of time they spend on domestic labour and childcare, mothers still put in more hours, with women spending twice as much time with their children compared to men. [xvi]

These findings highlight a persistent gender disparity in unpaid domestic labour and childcare, with working women and mothers still taking on the bulk of these responsibilities even as they have substantially increased their participation in the workforce.

For single working mothers, without a partner or support system they bear the entire load of household and parenting responsibilities, whilst navigating inflexible work environments, costly childcare and substantial financial constraints. In the UK, lone-parent families, mostly headed by women, account for 16% of families.[xvii] In the US, 80% of the 11 million single parent families are led by women,[xviii] with nearly 30% living below the poverty line. This additional work is rarely acknowledged, let alone compensated.

Mother's looking after children with additional needs also feel the impact of this labour. Taking on the lions-share of work in relation to managing the needs of their child, from scheduling hospital appointments, dealing with school support, managing meltdowns and navigating sensory needs.

As Kathryn, an L&D director shares: 'My daughter is autistic. Alongside the hospital appointments, there is the constant worry about school phone calls and having to deal with issues as they arise. I arrive to work stressed and can be on tenterhooks all day.' She adds: 'It's a constant, low-level worry. My mind is always strategising, and anticipating, always attempting to mitigate future risks. This worry is ever-present, adding extra stress.'

Experts suggest this invisible, unlimited work comes in three overlapping categories. [xix] However, through our own experiences, research and interviews, we have identified six pillars of invisible labour that disproportionately fall on women in both the home and workplace. While discussions around cognitive load, emotional labour and mental load have gained traction in recent years, we believe the physical, financial and vigilance burdens women carry must be acknowledged.

These **six invisible pillars** shape a woman's daily life, dictating how we manage a household, raise children, create wealth, remain safe and navigate professional spaces.

This framework is not just about the amount of work women take on, it's about how this work remains unseen, undervalued and unaccounted for in economic, professional and domestic spheres. It's about how these loads drain energy and power from women, preventing us from excelling in any sphere. Much of this labour is taken for granted, leading to burnout and resentment.

As Sam states: 'It's a barrier to gender equality in both work and home spaces.' We are aware that every partnership and household is different. This insight comes from our survey, our personal experiences, interviews and secondary research

Cognitive Labour - The Unseen Planning and Coordination
Cognitive labour is the constant mental tracking, organising, planning and prioritising required to manage daily life. It is mentally exhausting and takes up significant cognitive bandwidth. This unseen work ensures the smooth operation of both home and work, yet it is rarely acknowledged or shared equally.

In the Home:
- **Managing Family Schedules:** Tracking school events, extra-curricular activities, medical appointments, holiday planning, and social commitments.

- **Meal Planning & Grocery Shopping:** Deciding what to cook, ensuring food is stocked, making school lunches.
- **Household Logistics:** Coordinating home maintenance, childcare, cleaning schedules, knowing when cleaning supplies are running low, where they are stored.
- **Gift Buying, Giving & Special Occasions:** Remembering birthdays, Christmas, anniversaries and key events for extended family and friends

In Work:
- **Office Housekeeping:** Women are often the ones to remember colleagues' birthdays, plan team-building activities, or organise celebrations.
- **Team Morale Management:** Checking in on colleagues, ensuring everyone feels included, and fostering a positive environment.

Emotional Labour: The Invisible Management of Feelings

Emotional labour involves regulating one's own emotions while managing the emotions of others. It is often performed unconsciously and expected from women in a way that it is not from men.

In the Home:
- **Soothing Family Tensions:** Acting as the mediator between children, partners, and extended family members, ensuring harmony.

- **Anticipating and Managing Children's Mental Health Needs:** Supporting a child's anxiety, stress from school, sensory needs or friendship struggles.
- **Emotional Support for a Partner:** Many women become the primary emotional outlet for their spouse, providing a listening ear, encouragement, and emotional validation.
- **Caring for Aging Parents:** Checking in on elderly family members, coordinating their care, and providing emotional support.
- **Organising Couples Therapy:** Women are more likely to initiate therapy when facing relationship issues.

In Work:

- **"Office Mum" Role:** Women are more likely to be expected to handle emotional crises at work, providing emotional support to colleagues or mentoring junior employees.
- **Diplomatic Conflict Resolution:** Often, women are the ones expected to diffuse office tensions or soften workplace disputes, rather than confronting them head-on.
- **Performance of Professionalism:** Women are expected to manage their emotions carefully, assertiveness is often seen as aggression, while showing vulnerability can be perceived as incompetence.

Physical Labour: The Unpaid, Repetitive Work That Keeps Life Moving

Physical labour includes the hands-on, repetitive tasks that keep a household or workplace running. While some tasks are shared more equitably, many still disproportionately fall on women, especially tasks deemed less 'visible' or 'important'.

In the Home:

- **Housework:** Laundry, dishes, tidying up, organising clutter, and general cleaning.
- **Childcare Responsibilities:** Bathing, dressing, feeding, supervising, school runs, and middle-of-the-night wake-ups.
- **Elder Care:** Helping aging parents with daily tasks, from cooking to medical appointments and personal care.

In Work:

- **Office Housework:** Women often take on physical tasks in the workplace, such as setting up rooms for meetings, clearing up after events, or handling supplies.
- **Workplace Event Prep:** Women are more likely to be responsible for decorating, catering, and ensuring logistical details for team gatherings.

Health Labour: Personal and Family Health Advocacy and Management

Health labour refers to the tracking of medical needs - advocating for care and absorbing the emotional burden of health crises. It also refers to women managing their own healthcare needs, dealing with discrimination, medical gaslighting and poor diagnosis.

In the Home:
- **Family Health Management:** Scheduling, tracking and managing medical appointments, healthcare support plans, dietary and lifestyle needs - for children, partners, elderly relatives.
- **Health advocacy:** Researching treatments, pushing for treatment for necessary care when medical concerns are dismissed. Overcoming medical gaslighting for women's health challenges.

In Work:
- **Managing own health in silence:** Many women downplay physical and mental struggles to avoid discrimination or being perceived as weak or unreliable

Financial Labour: The Weight of Economic Responsibility
Financial labour refers to both earning and managing finances, ensuring economic stability for the household or team.

In the Home:
- **Budget Management:** Paying bills, tracking expenses, and managing financial planning for the household, overcontributing earnings to the running of the house.
- **Career Sacrifices:** Women are more likely to adjust their work hours, take career breaks, or accept lower-paying jobs to accommodate family needs.

- **The Cost of Invisible Work:** Many women forego self-care, upskilling, or leisure activities to ensure the family's financial stability.
- **Financial Anxiety:** In relation to managing household expenditure

In Work:
- **Underpaid & Overlooked Labour:** Women still face a gender pay gap and slower career progression, often doing more work for less pay.
- **HR and DEI Responsibilities:** Women disproportionately take on diversity and inclusion work, often unpaid or unrecognised.
- **Financial Planning & Oversight:** Ensuring office budgets, organising team events with minimal funds, and tracking departmental expenses. Women will often pay for presents and gifts from their own money or top up a gift fund.

Vigilance Labour - The burden of managing our personal safety

Vigilance labour refers to the mental and physical effort women undertake to protect their day-to-day safety against gender-based violence and harassment.

In the Home:
- **Digital Safety of Children:** Anecdotal evidence from our interviews, suggests women are more likely to monitor online behaviour and step into manage school bullying, cyberbullying and staying alert to online risks.

- **Home can be one of most dangerous places for women:** In 2023[xx], 51,000 women and girls were killed by an intimate partner or family member. In the UK, 74% of domestic abuse victims are female.

In Work and Public Spaces:

- **Situational Awareness:** Women have to assess surroundings in public spaces, avoid poorly lit areas and plan routes to minimise risk.
- **Safety precautions in Transport:** Sharing live locations, carrying keys between fingers, avoiding unsafe rideshares, assessing public transport seating and safety.
- **Workplace Harassment:** Women often feel responsible for managing and avoiding uncomfortable situations, managing unwanted attention or reporting inappropriate behaviour in professional settings.

This pervasive issue of 'thinking of everything' impedes our progress. When we are locked into lower-level tasks, we are unable to fulfil our purpose. We are not spending time on career progression or taking meaningful action towards our dreams and ambitions. In the home, this work remains a sensitive topic, simmering beneath the surface of many relationships. When broached, it can spark heated arguments, adding another layer to the already heavy load women bear.

Lisa, a mother of three and a senior Audit Officer in the Finance Sector, shares: 'It's sometimes easier to get on with it than to deal with potential conflict, especially after a really tough day at work.'

She adds: 'I deal with conflict all day long. I am exhausted and just want support when I get home. I don't want to nag, argue, or negotiate about who should do what or who has done more; nor do I want to be responsible for delegating tasks or telling someone what to do. I just want a partner who steps up, notices what needs to be done, and does it without being asked or requiring a thank you. Inevitably, that involves me just doing it.'

As we discussed 'invisible and emotional labour', with the women we interviewed, we found a further insight, the *recognition and reward* factor. It seems we are so desperately grateful for men's participation in domestic duties, we view any contribution as exceptional, leading to expressions of gratitude that are not equally extended to us for the same tasks.

That big sink full of dirty dishes that gets washed every day by a wife often goes unnoticed by a husband, zero gratitude expressed, but there is an expectation that it is done. But when the husband does it, many of our interviewees shared they often gushed effusive thanks.

In *The Second Shift: Working Parents and the Revolution in the Home* Arlie Hochschild introduces the 'economy of gratitude' theory, which suggests that appreciation within relationships plays a crucial role in shaping the division of household labour. When contributions - particularly domestic and emotional labour - go unnoticed or unacknowledged, resentment builds, reinforcing unequal workload.

Jess Alberts and Angela Trethewey's research[xxi] supports this, showing that the absence of gratitude is not just an oversight but an active force in sustaining traditional gender roles. While men are often praised for minimal contributions, women's unpaid labour is treated as an unspoken expectation rather than necessity, deepening the imbalance Hochschild identified.

This dynamic aligns with John and Julie Gottman's research on relationship stability, particularly their identification of contempt as one of the most corrosive factors in partnerships. When one partner consistently feels unappreciated, unresolved grievances and emotional neglect can fester, eroding intimacy, communication, and mutual respect.

Over time, an imbalanced division of labour - paired with a lack of acknowledgment - fuels resentment, making gratitude not just a sign of fairness but an essential safeguard against relational breakdown.

Research consistently shows that a woman's marital satisfaction and sense of fairness are directly tied to a man's participation in routine housework. Far from being a minor issue, shared domestic responsibility plays a crucial role in sustaining long-term, healthy relationships.

The reality is that the many micro-tasks women undertake daily remain unseen and, therefore undervalued by their spouses - we call this the 'Awareness Gap'. research by the Pew Center,[xxii] found US men tend to overestimate their contributions to housework and childcare, while women feel their efforts are undervalued.

It's this disconnect that fuels frustration and burnout and ultimately the contempt that the Gottman's identified in relationships. Women's domestic labour is frequent, time sensitive, daily, sometimes hourly, and it prevents women from downtime, rest and relaxation, pursuing 'me-time', or maintaining friendships. Men's domestic labour is weekly, often sporadic or rare tasks, such as taking bins out, washing a car or mowing a lawn - none of which are time sensitive or daily. This provides men with more time to relax, pursue hobbies and go out with friends.

During the pandemic, the term 'Weaponised Incompetence' amassed over 148 million views on social media platform, TikTok. The term describes a behaviour, in which one partner pretends to be bad at simple tasks, avoids learning to do them well or fails to take the initiative to evade responsibility - a form of learned helplessness. While social media often jokes about men's contributions to household chores, the reality is far more complex.

In our conversations with the women we interviewed, it was the constant expectation that as women we know the minute-by-minute location of laundry, a glue stick, or where the trash bags are located. When this is multiplied by 2 or even 3 additional individuals (aka children), it becomes exhausting, a constant stock taking exercise.

'Your husband is not your child,' Farah states very strongly. This critical point highlights the need for a deeper understanding and equitable distribution of household responsibilities. 'Increasingly, I see women in various stages of life, whether they are pursuing high-powered careers or are stay-at-home mothers, who take on the role of looking after their husbands or partners as if they were another child. You are not their mother. You are their partner, and your job is not to follow them around, clean up their messes, or ensure everything is in order. You shouldn't even do this for your children if they are old enough to clean up after themselves, let alone for a grown-up partner.'

The necessity for reminders becomes another layer of emotional labour, frequently leading to the all-too-familiar refrain of 'I'll do it later.' This response, and the delay it implies, often becomes a source of contention within relationships.

In a 2022 HuffPost article, Sarah Spencey Northey, a marriage and family therapist, says: 'On a surface level, it looks like you're just nagging about chores to a person who 'defers' to your competence. But on a deeper level, you're experiencing not being able to trust and turn to your partner for support.'[xxiii]

At its worst, in abusive relationships, it can create a severe imbalance of power, where people may use it manipulate their partners and maintain control over them. At best, it results in needs not being met. In time, it affects relationships, creating imbalance, resentment a lack of trust, conflict and communication breakdown and emotional disconnection.

In one of her viral videos, researcher and storyteller, Brené Brown[xxiv] shared a crucial perspective on partnership and support within a relationship. She suggests that dividing tasks and responsibilities isn't always a matter of equal halves; it's unrealistic to expect a perpetual 50-50 split. There will be days when one partner can only give 30%, necessitating the other to step up with 70% to keep the household functioning optimally. This fluidity in contribution is an essential insight for maintaining harmony and support in a partnership.

However, our survey highlighted that women are picking up 70% of household responsibilities, a dynamic Eve Rodsky calls the 'shefault' in her book, *Fair Play*. The key here is setting boundaries, communicating who can pick up what and distributing workload equally, agreeing a framework to live by that benefits everyone.

The pandemic created another domestic labour inequality touchpoint. Pre-Covid, the research showed the gap between men's and women's domestic hours modestly closing, although this was largely attributable to women doing less rather than men doing more. However, research conducted during the pandemic, showed a widening inequality in terms of unpaid work in the home with more women shouldering the burden of care, schooling and often having to reduce their own paid work to support children.[xxv]

Jacqueline, a marketing executive at a Seattle based tech giant, shares her recollections: 'Initially, my partner started to do a little more, but very quickly the burden fell to me to ensure schooling was done, food was cooked, and the house was cleaned. We now both work from home most of the week and I will put the laundry on during a coffee break or take the dog out for a quick walk before work, or even make the dinner during my lunch break, he will rest.'

She adds: 'He even gets up later now and literally jumps out of bed at 8.45 and into his office, meanwhile, I've been up since 5.30 a.m., trying to cram in fitness, getting kids and myself ready for school and work.'

Women don't just shoulder the invisible labour of childcare and housework - they also take on the bulk of eldercare, especially women aged 50+. A 2020 Office of National Statistics (UK)[xxvi] survey found that midlife women are more likely to be informal carers, often juggling full-time work, senior roles, school-age children, and menopause.

A 2014 study by the American Sociological Association (ASA), found daughters provide an average of 12.3 hours of eldercare per month compared to sons' 5.6 hours.[xxvii] Sons reduce their caregiving efforts when they have sisters, while daughters increase theirs if they have a brother - suggesting sons pass these responsibilities onto women. Research also shows women suffer more health and financial-related consequences from elder care with some studies linking it to higher mortality rates.[xxviii]

This division of daily tasks does more than reflect individual household dynamics; it echoes the broader societal assumptions that shape our interactions. Take, for instance, the protocols within our educational institutions. When a child-related concern arises, the default protocol often directs the communication towards the mother. Is there an underlying assumption that mothers are more available, or that their professional commitments are secondary?

Farah recounts a revealing encounter that brings this issue to light: While picking up her children from school, a conversation with a male staff member led to a surprising revelation. Accustomed to seeing her husband handle the school runs, the staff member had formed the impression that he was a single father. 'Oh, I didn't realise he was married; we never see you,' he remarked upon seeing Farah.

This assumption speaks volumes about the societal scripts we follow. It suggests that when a father is present in scenarios typically dominated by mothers, the default assumption skews towards single parenthood. Would a mother ever be viewed through the same lens, or are such assumptions exclusively reserved for fathers?

This encounter not only highlights the unequal expectations placed on women but also exposes the stereotypes that fathers face when they step into roles traditionally assigned to mothers.

Scandinavian countries have long championed gender equality in parenting, with fatherhood encompassing a full spectrum of childcare and household responsibilities. Sweden embodies this progressive shift, offering parents 480 days of paid leave, with fathers claiming about 30%.

Unlike in many societies where paternal involvement in caregiving is viewed as an exception, in Scandinavia, it is a cultural norm. Fathers on paternity leave are a common sight, pushing strollers, attending parent groups, and taking an active role in their children's formative years. These policies do more than support families; they reshape society, dismantle gendered roles, and influence children's perceptions of shared responsibilities.

While some cultures might perceive a father's decision to take paternity leave as a lack of ambition or an aberration from the norm, in Scandinavia, it is a testament to a father's commitment to his family and society's commitment to supporting that choice.

The benefits of such policies extend beyond the individual families; they are reflective of a society that understands the long-term advantages of a well-balanced home environment and how that can support both men and women in 'achieving their all'. Children grow up with the model of shared responsibilities and mutual support, which influences their own perceptions of gender roles. Moreover, it contributes to the dismantling of stigmas around 'traditional' roles, allowing both men and women to pursue their professional ambitions without sacrificing their familial roles.

Farah expresses a critical insight: 'I am a firm believer that sharing these nuanced yet important day-to-day activities within a household can lead to a societal shift. This seemingly small yet profound practice has the potential to create ripples of change, advancing gender equality not just for our generation but for those who will follow.'

We must teach our boys that domestic duties are an equal responsibility. This can be challenging when they don't see men modelling this behaviour, either in their homes or on TV. Too often, the burden of teaching emotional intelligence, household skills, communication, empathy, and care falls on women - another form of invisible emotional labour.

For fathers, embracing modern masculinity means championing equality at home and at work. Capitalism and patriarchy harm men as much as women. In her coaching, Sam sees the impact of conditioning that demands men "be strong" and never show weakness". She notes: 'Men are struggling just as much as women. We need open communication - not just to highlight women's challenges but to include men in the conversation too, acknowledge all our experiences and find solutions.'

Many men we talked to expressed feeling pushed out or unable to get things right. Encouraging shared responsibility at home means women must allow men to engage fully, avoiding 'maternal gatekeeping' - where mothers, consciously or unconsciously, limit fathers' involvement in parenting. While often driven by frustration or habit, it can also fuel a cycle of withdrawal, where women assume more responsibilities, leading men to disengage - ultimately causing burnout and resentment.

Research shows traditional gender beliefs reinforce gatekeeping, positioning mothers as primary caregivers. While increased paternal involvement alleviates mothers' burdens, it may also challenge women's identity and sense of authority in parenting. Ruth Gaunt's research[xxix] suggests women with lower self-esteem, may view motherhood as a source of validation and control, making them reluctant to share responsibilities. Shame and guilt are factors here too, the pressure to be the perfect mother, wife and high achiever push women into over-drive, trapping them in be-it all and do-it all modes.

Studies have shown there are other dynamics at play too. In their paper the Integrative Theory of Domestic Labour,[xxx] Alberts, Tracy & Tretheway introduced the concept of levels - the idea that people have different tolerances for household disorder. Women, often having a lower threshold for mess or unfinished tasks, step in first. Over time, they become default managers of the household, this reinforces gender expectations, and they end up becoming the experts of doing it all.

Our survey responses provided further nuance in this fraught issue. Men often ask, "Just tell me what you want me to do" or "Write me a list, and I'll do it," then fail to understand the emotional reaction that follows. The answer? These questions are still a form of invisible labour. Women don't have the luxury of someone else planning, delegating, or writing a step-by-step execution plan for them - yet they're expected to do it for their partners. True equality at home isn't about men "helping" women - it's about men owning their share of the cognitive and physical load - without instruction - as much as it's about women letting men in.

Emotional labour & invisible work are not just confined to the home - they operate insidiously in the workplace too.
Sam shares an example from six years ago: 'As the only woman in a senior leadership team, I attended an offsite where a male colleague messaged me for hotel details and event timings - all of which were in an email he had received 3 days prior. When I jokingly asked why he hadn't asked anyone else, he replied, "Ah, but the women always know the details - just like my wife."'

This assumption that women naturally handle logistics, communication, and emotional management mirrors the broader inequality of emotional labour. However, it's not just about low-level tasks; women's career paths are littered with obstacles. The 'Broken Rung' sees fewer women promoted to managerial roles, while the 'Glass Ceiling' remains an invisible barrier blocking advancement to top leadership.

When women do reach leadership, they must constantly negotiate their presence in a male-coded space. They must be confident but not arrogant, strong but not aggressive, competent but not intimidating. Their voices, looks, and even parenting choices are scrutinised in ways men never experience. Eagly and Karau's Role Incongruity Theory[xxxi] explains how women face backlash when displaying strong leadership traits, as they contradict gender norms. Leadership is linked to assertiveness, decisiveness, and dominance, while women are expected to embody nurturing, empathy, and support - creating an impossible mismatch.

Double Bind Theory[xxxii] takes this further. Women must toggle between conflicting expectations, too strong and they're seen as unlikeable, too warm and they're dismissed as weak. A 2024[xxxiii] report found 76% of high performing women receive negative feedback compared to 2% of men. Feedback for men is often competency based, whereas women receive commentary on their style or personality. For Black women, this scrutiny intensifies as they navigate the triple bind of gender, race, and class.

This relentless pressure can lead to Queen Bee Syndrome,[xxxiv] where some women distance themselves from female peers or adopt male-coded norms to survive. Having fought their way up, they may unconsciously uphold the very system that oppressed them, believing younger female colleagues must also "prove themselves." This isn't about individual betrayal - it's a symptom of a system that pits women against each other, making collaboration difficult.

Alex, a sales director, shares her experience of this in her company: 'We were excited when our first female CEO was appointed, but she immediately surrounded herself with an all-male leadership team. She refused to engage in anything gender-related, like mentoring women, and spoke only of her gratitude to her male sponsors. It was such a missed opportunity and left many women in the business feeling frustrated and let down.'

Sam shares this perspective: 'This behaviour is a wounded type of leadership. After decades of battling discrimination, many women in leadership internalise the struggle. We develop protective, survival strategies, but these can be self-limiting and divisive. This is a by-product of a structure that forces women to leader in a way that contradicts innate strengths.'

Unlike men, women are not permitted to 'just lead' - they are required to carefully curate how they lead to fit in and survive. This behaviour is linked to Impression management theory[xxxv] where individuals consciously and unconsciously shape others' perceptions of them. Women may adopt masculine traits or soften their tone, over-apologise, hold back ideas or downplay intelligence to appear less threatening.

Leila's story is a great example of the tightrope women walk between likeability and competence. As the Executive Assistant to a CEO, she recalls how a new male CEO targeted strong female leaders: 'After one-on-ones with two female leaders, he came out of his office and told me he disliked how they came across - "too pushy." Both left the company soon after as he launched a campaign against them. The impact was twofold, we lost two great leaders, and the women who stayed started editing themselves into a version of female leadership he deemed acceptable. It was only the women leaders who were punished in this way.'

These experiences lead to disempowered leadership for women, what we refer to as wounded feminine leadership. Rooted in suppressed feminine energy, it creates self-doubt, imposter syndrome, people-pleasing or being conflict avoidant. Women in wounded feminine leadership often overcompensate by working harder.

The weight of this constant cognitive load is crushing. Is it any wonder women are burning out at alarming rates? Or our leadership tenure is cut short? Women leaders don't just run businesses, they navigate invisible barriers daily, raise families, and shoulder a disproportionate share of unpaid and undervalued labour. Their male counterparts move freely, unencumbered by these expectations.

Now, imagine how unstoppable we would be if we didn't have to fight these battles.

In 2005, Michelle Ryan and Alexander Haslam identified the 'Glass Cliff.' [xxxvi] This term describes how women are disproportionately placed in leadership roles during a crisis. Ironically, in these crisis moments, it's women's feminine or communal traits - empathy, support, nurturing, collaboration - that are seen as critical.

It seems women are parachuted into these positions only to be judged more harshly, given less support and quickly replaced, usually by men. When the glass cliff shatters, it reinforces the myth that women are unfit to lead. Their research also found that when companies are thriving, leadership roles disproportionately go to men.

This pattern mirrors the Fall of Eve narrative, where a woman is positioned in a precarious situation and then blamed for the outcome. Just as Eve's choice led to banishment and suffering, women in leadership today are set up to fail, then held accountable for systemic failures beyond their control.

The scarcity of leadership opportunities for women can create another dynamic, fuelling competition between women rather than collaboration. Defensiveness replaces solidarity. Women are not fighting each other by choice, they are fighting for survival in a system that still resists their presence.

Instead of lifting one another up, women in leadership are pitted against each other, reinforcing the false belief that women can't lead effectively. The result? A self-perpetuating cycle where women's leadership remains an exception, not the norm, and true equality stays out of reach.
The real problem isn't women. It's the system that forces us to compete for scraps. Women aren't failing at leadership. Leadership is failing women.

We hope this chapter sparks conversations. Women's invisible labour holds society together, yet it remains unseen, undervalued and unaccounted for, because our societies undervalue our contribution. At home we shoulder the bulk of domestic labour, childcare and mental load. At work we navigate double standards, bias and discrimination. As we land in leadership roles, we are offered little support, often set up to fail, expected to lead like a man and then punished when we do. Despite six decades of women driving economic progress, our needs remain unmet. The system is not designed for us - it is designed to extract from us.

Women are not failing; society is consistently failing women. It is time to make the invisible visible and demand change.

Notes for Male Allies

This chapter highlights the hidden labour women carry at home and work. Reflect on how often you see women taking on more, whether by default or necessity. Do you truly share the load, or does she handle the majority? Do you value her contributions equally to yours, or do you find yourself saying, *"Just tell me what you want me to do,"* or *"Write me a list and I'll do it"*? If you lead a male allies group, discuss how invisible labour shapes family and work life - true allyship means taking responsibility, not just appreciating the effort.

As a leader, consider how much emotional labour women in your organisation manage. Are you unconsciously penalising them for stepping outside invisible expectations?

Pause and Reflect

How aware are you of the emotional and mental labour you contribute at home and work? Which areas feel most burdensome, and how might you communicate or redistribute these responsibilities?

In what ways have your beliefs about control or perfection influenced how responsibilities are divided? What would happen if you allowed others to take ownership, even imperfectly? Are you feeling guilt and shame and taking on more than you need?

In the workplace develop an abundance mindset, focus on lifting women up. Develop your authentic leadership style to prevent self-editing. Struggling with Imposter syndrome? Dose up on self-compassion to mitigate self-doubt. Delegate strategically to set boundaries and avoid cognitive overload.

'For too long, the responsibility for managing home and family has fallen unequally on women. It's time for that to change'.
— *Michelle Obama*

Chapter Three
The Impact of the Myth

It is time to set aside idealised notions and face the harsh truth; the pressure to live up to the myth is taking its toll on all women.

For many of the women who responded to our survey, 'having it all' is a contentious topic, several of them expressed frustration over the unrealistic expectations it placed on them. For most, the phrase symbolises a standard of perfection that is not only unattainable but deeply rooted in systemic inequalities and persistent gender biases.

The following quotes from our survey reflect the personal and professional toll this myth has exacted on women, highlighting their lived experiences and the challenges they face in balancing societal and personal expectations:

- 'It equates to an unattainable standard of perfection; women very rightly can now do "it all" but lack support in many areas and still have to manage unfair views'.

'It's the definition of success for a working mother. It's an impossible standard'.

'When I became a mother, I had to return to work before Mat Leave finished as we financially couldn't afford for me to stay off any longer. Having constant working mother's guilt for not being at home, whilst trying to manage a really demanding job. It was very stressful and none of my male bosses understood as they had stay at home wives'.

It is our belief that the cost to professional women is significant in all aspects of our lives, physical and mental health, financial and personal.

Building on this discussion, let's compare how different generations, Generation Z, Millennials, Generation X, and Baby Boomers, navigate these challenges. Each generation faces unique pressures and has developed distinct approaches to work-life balance and self-awareness.

Generation Z is entering the workforce with a strong emphasis on flexibility, mental health, and digital fluency. They value diversity, inclusivity, and social responsibility in their workplaces, often seeking out employers who align with their values. Gen Z is vocal about the importance of mental health and is less willing to compromise personal well-being for career advancement. They often challenge traditional work structures and advocate for work-life integration rather than balance. While their emphasis on mental health and work satisfaction is progressive, it can also lead to anxiety and stress when their high standards are not met.[xxxvii]

Millennials often strive for a career that is deeply intertwined with their personal identity and values. They are more likely to prioritise job satisfaction and purpose over traditional markers of success like salary or title. However, this can also lead to heightened self-criticism and guilt when they fail to meet their own expectations in both their personal and professional lives. Many Millennials report feeling a constant need to prove themselves in both arenas, leading to burnout.[xxxviii]

Generation X tends to uphold a pragmatic approach to work-life balance, perhaps because they grew up in a transforming workplace, where the household shifted from one working parent to two. This generation is more likely to emphasise the importance of boundaries between work and personal life than Millennials. However, they often struggle with the guilt of not giving enough to either domain, caught between the increasing demands of aging parents and their own children.[xxxix]

Baby Boomers have traditionally placed a strong emphasis on work as a central part of their identity, with a focus on loyalty and long hours as markers of success. As they move towards retirement, many Boomers reflect on their careers in terms of achievements and time spent, which can lead to regrets about not having spent enough time on personal life or self-care.[xl]

Each generation's approach offers valuable lessons on the importance of self-awareness and the need to balance personal fulfillment with professional achievements. This intergenerational view not only emphasises the evolving nature of work-life challenges but also points to the shifting paradigms in how different ages perceive and react to the pressures of maintaining identity and success.

Gender Myths and Emotional Labour's Mental Toll

In our survey, we were shocked and saddened by how many respondents experienced burnout trying to do it all and be it all. This is backed up by a 2022 Deloitte paper; it found that 40% of women cite burnout as a reason for leaving their career. In Deloitte's most recent 2024 study,[xli] it states: 'Half of the women, describe their stress levels as higher than a year ago and half of women who live with a partner and have children at home bear the most responsibility for childcare.'

Burnout is a state of mental, emotional and physical exhaustion brought on by prolonged or repeated stress. As Psychology Today[xlii] states: 'Burnout is not simply a result of working long hours or juggling too many tasks…. The cynicism, depression and lethargy that are characteristic of burnout most often occur when a person is not in control of how a job is carried out, at work or at home.'

Left unattended, burnout can have serious health consequences. Burnout is also more prevalent in people with perfectionist and people-pleasing tendencies.

A study conducted by Great Places to Work and Maven,[xliii] found that mothers in the US in paid employment are 23% more likely to experience burnout than fathers in paid employment. Burnout sneaks quietly into the lives of those juggling the demands of motherhood and a professional career. It's a silent echo of the struggle to 'have it all, do it all and be it all', a battle cry for the modern woman striving to fulfil every role with grace and vigour.

It also frays the edges of relationships and chips away at emotional wellbeing and physical health. When the scales tip, everything from intimate partnerships to daily tasks becomes a herculean effort. It cuts through everything, impacting relationships, ability to work and even the ability to parent. Yet, we seem to have created a world where burnout is seen as a rite of passage.

In this high-wire act, the role of a supportive partner is crucial. Women report a spectrum of supportiveness, ranging from partners who are pillars of strength to those who, perhaps caught in their own whirlwind, add to the burden. Similarly, workplaces oscillate between being sanctuaries of support to arenas of indifference and ignorance.

According to a 2022 study entitled *Double Jeopardy: The roles of Job Autonomy & Spousal Gender Ideology in Employed Women's Mental Health*[xliv] identified that a quarter of working women in the UK reported being unable to manage job stress. The report sought to understand whether it's the lack of job autonomy (job related stress and burnout) or the gender division of household labour that affects women's mental health. The research argues both are at play at the same time. Women suffer a double jeopardy; they lack job autonomy and had traditional husbands and therefore took on the lion's share of household duties and caring responsibilities.

The Lancet[xlv] conducted a review of 19 studies to understand the impact of gender/unpaid labour and mental health. Acknowledging the lack of research to date, it found that unpaid labour is associated with poorer mental health in women, but the effects were less apparent for men. Interestingly, it also noted the severe lack of analysis conducted on this issue, a telling insight we consistently see when it comes to research and reporting into women's health.

The UK government is so sufficiently concerned, it made improving women's mental health a public health priority. A 2021 BMJ article[xlvi] shared how highly stressful unpaid labour is for women, causing high levels of cortisol, leading to physical and emotional distress, depression and anxiety, feelings of devaluation, isolation, loneliness and resentment. Typically, women do more of the time sensitive, high-schedule control jobs in the home versus men, this jobs often have a direct impact on cortisol.

In addition, providing long-term or high intensity care for a sick or elderly relative has been associated with an excess of mental health disorders in women[xlvii].

The Myth's Impact on Physical Health

When our mental health suffers, our physical health follows. As we have shifted from a production to services-based economy, there is a corresponding increase in exposure of employees to varying degrees of stress from toxic cultures. Employees are expected to manage and suppress their emotional states to carry out their job responsibilities in a professional manner. [xlviii] More and more, employees are rewarded based on their ability to 'emotionally labour'.

Multiple studies[xlix] have shown that emotional labour in the workplace can lead to serious health issues, high blood pressure, heart disease, and emotional trauma. Experts widely acknowledge that the way societal structures and gender norms intersect plays a significant role in women's decreasing health, culminating in the gender health gap.

Cardiovascular disease (CVD) is the #1 killer of women. Over the past decade, the prevalence of CVD risk factors has increased in women and progressively more in younger women than ever before.[l] Chronic stress weakens the immune system, increases inflammation and some cancers.

Women face a higher risk of developing Alzheimer's disease and tend to experience more severe clinical and pathological progression with early onset dementia. In contrast men are at greater risk of developing vascular dementia. While longevity predisposes women's susceptibility to Alzheimer's, biological and lifestyle factors play a role. Sleep deprivation is a major contributor - research from Harvard suggests getting less than six hours sleep per night or experiencing fragmented sleep increases levels of beta-amyloid, a hallmark of Alzheimer's disease.[li]

Inadequate sleep during midlife further raises the risk of dementia with shift work, care-giving responsibilities, anxiety and demanding careers disrupting sleep patterns. Menopausal women are 40% more likely to suffer from insomnia, and twice as likely to be diagnose with anxiety and depression. These health disparities show urgent need for better health policies, stronger support systems, and more research focused on women's health.

Women have up to a fourfold increase in risk for autoimmune disease compared to men. Autoimmune disorders tend to affect women during periods of extensive stress and hormonal change, such as pregnancy or menopause.

This is an area where women often experience the most medical invalidation as they are so hard to diagnose and treat. Several researchers believe there are genetic factors related to autoimmune disorders. However, there is a growing body of work that is questioning whether different mental states can positively or negatively affect biological functioning. A large meta-analysis of 300 independent studies published over 30 years indicated psychological stress was associated with the suppression of the immune system.[lii]

The painful reality is that many of the women we surveyed and interviewed consistently 'put themselves last', failing to eat properly, neglecting exercise, sacrificing rest and sleep in a bid to manage the hours of the dual burden.

For many, even seeking out healthcare is an additional tax on their time. Women described the exhausting process of having their concerns dismissed - mental and physical conditions, such as depression or endometriosis are often ignored, forcing women to fight repeatedly for medical acknowledgement and support. Research by McKinsey, there is a gender health gap, as women spend 25% more time in poor health compared to men, yet female illness continues to be under-researched.[liii]

Beyond the toll on physical health, many women are still unsafe in their own homes, with domestic violence continuing to be a devasting reality. For us, the evidence is clear: modern society is failing women, and in too many cases, it is killing them.

Financial Health and Stability

Since the 1970s, women's increasing participation in the labour force has been a major driver of economic growth. In the U.S, women's contributions were projected to add $3.5 trillion to the GDP by 2024[liv], with a potential $5.7 trillion gain over the next decade if female workforce participation continues to rise.

Despite this undeniable economic impact, systemic barriers persist, limiting women's financial independence and wealth creation. According to Moody Analytics, 'Limited and divergent progress has been made in elevating women in the workplace over the past decade,[lv] leaving women primed to miss out on potential wage and income gains.

The technology sector is a good example of this disparity. While Artificial Intelligence is expected to generate billions in economic value, women remain underrepresented in all roles in the tech sector, especially executive roles, and especially in AI. Furthermore, women receive just 2% of Venture Capital Funding to start up organisations.[lvi] This means women stand to lose out on the significant prospective wealth opportunity this inevitable tech bubble will deliver.

Following the pandemic, the UN warned gender equality would be set back by decades. The impact of quiet quitting, resignation rates, redundancy programmes and now return to office mandates threatening a woman's ability to earn.

Research by the London School of Economics shows men are four times as likely as women to be among those with very high incomes, with women still only making up 19.4% of the top 1% of earners in the UK. According to the UK's Women's Budget Group, women earn 30% less than men, carry out 60% more unpaid work and accumulate only half the private pension wealth that men do.[lvii]

Through our research and conversations with women, we identified a troubling pattern. A lack of control over their own money. Several women told us their earnings, and disposable income are managed or decided upon by their partner. Financial disagreements are a prevalent source of conflict in relationships. According to a 2019 study by the Institute for Divorce Financial Analysts,[lviii] financial issues are cited as the third leading cause of divorce, following infidelity and incompatibility.

The pressure on women's salaries doesn't stop there; studies indicate women spend 60% of their income on family expenses compared to men's 30%.[lix] This leaves women disproportionately saddled with daily costs, and vulnerable to future financial insecurity as they are unable to save or invest at the same rate as their partner. Farah shares a refrain that echoed throughout numerous conversations she had with women. 'Many women find themselves in financial arrangements where their income becomes the default source for day-to-day expenses, such as childcare, groceries, days out, pocket money, dinner money - the list goes on. Meanwhile, their partner's income is preserved as a safety net.'

One of the women we interviewed shared this: 'I contribute every penny to the household, while my partner says he's "saving for us". But I can't help wondering, what about me, what happens if we divorce or split up? I have no personal savings and am unable to save because all my income is spent on immediate outgoings.'

This imbalance often extends to decision-making dynamics. Even in dual-income households, women are more likely to manage day-to-day budgets while men control long-term financial planning and investments. Research highlights a persistent gender gap in household investment decisions,[lx] where 'men often wield greater influence, even when their female partners are more risk-averse'. These biases further compound wealth gaps, leaving women vulnerable to financial insecurity. For stay-at-home mothers, the risks are even higher, as many are excluded from financial decision-making entirely, placing them at significant risk during life's uncertainties.

An interviewee who wished to remain anonymous shared her experiences. We'll call her Katie. A mum of two young boys, she works full-time in a middle management position, her partner is self-employed. Despite both working Katie picks up the slack in terms of managing their budget, constantly worried about making ends meet. Her partner contributes money when he can but is notoriously bad at managing finances. 'I can't rely on him; I budget all my income to support us. There have been numerous times when debt collectors turned up at the door, and I had to pay them off.'

Katie's situation is far from unique, the Young Women's Trust[lxi] found that in 2020, 1 in 10 young women reported experiencing economic abuse. This abuse can involve exerting influence over education, training, and employment, preventing them from studying, stopping them having a job or earning money, taking wages, and refusing to pay child support.

She continues: 'Any discussion about money turns into a war. Recently, I asked him to contribute more to our monthly outgoings due to the cost-of-living crisis. He claimed that he was saving for his pension, and he had his new car payments - an investment he didn't discuss with me. Rather than offering solutions, he started to shout at me to stop wasting food. He wanted to look at the bills as if I was lying about the cost of electricity. It's exhausting. My family asks me why I am still married, but he is a good dad to our children, and I can't afford to live on my own.'

Financial abuse isn't always overt, but its consequences are severe. Like many women, Katie faces an impossible choice - staying in an unfair financial situation or risk greater instability.

Kim Kiyosaki's book *Rich Woman* presents sobering statistics that are a wake-up call to the reality many women deal with, even decades after the book first published:[lxii]

- 47% of women over the age of 50 are single.
- 50% of marriages end in divorce.
- In the first year after a divorce, a woman's standard of living drops an average of 73%.
- Of the elderly living in poverty, 3 out of 4 are women, 80% of whom were not poor when their husbands were alive.
- Nearly 7 out of 10 women will at some time live in poverty.

These are not just numbers; they are stories, a warning and a call to action. Financial literacy and independence are not luxuries for women - they are necessities.

Sam reflects on this reality from two deeply personal perspectives: 'My mum had a fraught relationship with money.

As a single parent family, there wasn't a lot of it. Money was to be spent, rarely invested or saved. It was simply about surviving. Her experiences with money taught me to fear it for a very long time,' she shares. 'It wasn't until I met Audrey, a wonderful 86-year-old who I shopped for during the pandemic, that I realised how essential financial knowledge was for women's empowerment. She had come from very little wealth but had learnt to invest and take ownership of her financial future.'

As with many of our stories, they highlight how money is not just currency, it is freedom, power and the ability to choose the life you want.

The Gender Pay & Wealth Gaps
We can't discuss financial health without addressing the *Gender Pay and Wealth Gaps*, which continue to limit women's financial independence and security. As women age, insufficient financial resources lead to deteriorating health and quality of life, and in some cases, increased homelessness - this is currently happening in Australia.

The Global Gender Gap report of 2023 by the World Economic Forum benchmarks 146 countries on their progress towards gender parity across four key dimensions: Economic Participation and Opportunity, Educational Attainment, Health and Survival, and Political Empowerment. The report highlights that the global gender gap has closed by 68.4%, with just a 0.3 percentage point improvement from the previous year.[lxiii] Globally, women earn 77 cents for every dollar earned by men. However, analysts project it will take approximately 169 years to achieve full gender parity.[lxiv] The US pay gap widened for the first time in 20 years in 2023, marking a troubling setback in progress.

Unconscious bias contributes to the Gender Pay Gap, studies show that women who become parents suffer from the 'Motherhood Penalty', while men who become parents benefit from the 'Fatherhood Bonus', particularly in leadership positions.[lxv]

Women who become parents:
- Are routinely perceived as being less competent and committed
- Have fewer professional development opportunities
- Often receive less pay

Men who become parents:[lxvi]
- Are viewed as more reliable and stable
- Accelerate their careers
- Regularly receive more pay

The Gender Wealth Gap refers to the difference in assets owned by men and women and has a particular impact on women at retirement. Globally, women hold about 33% of world's wealth and according to research from World Economic Forum, women globally are expected to accumulate only 74% of the wealth men have.[lxvii]

A 2023 article in the New Statesmen brings into sharp focus the impact on women in the UK, citing research from the Women's Budget group, that found a 28% wealth gap between men and women aged 35 – 44, rising to an astonishing 42% by the age of 64. The UK's Office for National Statistics data revealed a 90% gender gap in private pension wealth and a 177% disparity in the average value of UK shares held by men and women.

This gendered economic inequality is painfully evident in the UK WASPI (Women Against State Pension Inequality) crisis, where millions of women born in the 1950s in the UK were blindsided by rapid pension age increases without adequate notice. Many of these women had already left the workforce, made financial plans based on the expected pension age of 60, and were suddenly left without the income they had relied on.

According to the Bank of America, the Great Wealth Transfer will see women inherit up to $30 trillion in the next decade. Yet this influx of wealth will not guarantee economic equality - because the gender wealth gap is so vast. While women may control more financial assets in the future, many may still lack true financial power. Limited financial literacy, coupled with gatekeeping in male-dominated financial institutions, continues to restrict our access to wealth-building opportunities. Inheritance alone will not close the gap - structural change in financial education and access is essential.

The UK's Women's Budget Group perceives that 'wealth inequality is gendered because of the unequal distribution of unpaid care and structural discrimination against women'.[lxviii]

Motherhood is one of the main reasons. A gap starts to widen, as mothers tend to reduce their hours to assume primary caregiving responsibility. The same report highlights that a woman's savings are typically exhausted first in heterosexual relationships due to the costs of childcare and care responsibilities. As the report states, 'unpaid care is at the heart of women's economic inequality'.[lxix]

In Europe about 33% of women take a career break for at least 6 months compared with 1% of men and 30% of women work part-time compared to 8% of men, to look after children.[lxx] Furthermore, shared parental leave is severely under-utilised by fathers - since 2015, less than 2% of new fathers in the UK accessed the scheme.

Childcare is another significant financial burden for families, particularly in the UK, which has some of the most expensive childcare in the world. These high costs deter women from returning to work and further entrench economic inequality. Elder care also limits women's ability to earn, as more women reduce their hours or resign their positions to care for aging parents.[lxxi].

For us, the evidence is undeniable - the myth of having it all, was never about empowering women - it has been about exhausting them. It's a system that is designed to extract maximum labour, emotionally, physically, and professionally, whilst offering minimal support and recognition.

The pursuit of 'having it all, doing it all and being it all' forces women into systems that are fundamentally rigged against them. This relentless chase often feels like navigating a modern-day Hunger Games, with obstacles like broken rungs, glass ceilings, cliffs, parenthood stigmas, gender pay and wealth gaps, emotional labour, the second shift, and health inequalities creating an almost insurmountable battlefield. Women are expected to work twice as hard for half the reward while meeting impossibly high standards in every facet of life.

Yet, this myth does not just harm women - it creates a double bind that limits both genders. While women are overloaded, men are trapped by rigid social stigma surrounding vulnerability and emotional expression. Globally, the suicide rate is more than twice as high amongst men and are more likely to struggle in silence, experiencing heightened stress, loneliness and mental health crises.

For too long gender roles have functioned as cages, restricting women's autonomy whilst isolating men from emotional connection. True progress will only come when we dismantle these restrictive ideals and collectively build frameworks that genuinely support us all.

By rejecting the myth of having it all not just for women, but for themselves as well, men can help create a culture where everyone can thrive without being crushed under unrealistic expectations.

Notes for Male Allies

Consider the distribution of labour in your household, is it fair? How often do you create space for shared decision making? Does your partner instigate or delegate most of the chore-sharing? Do you feel comfortable stepping into caregiving roles?

Discuss the impact of doing it all and being it all is having on your partner and the family. Look at the *Fair Play* framework and see how you can implement this in your house. It's normal to feel powerful emotions, spend time reflecting what you may struggle with in relation to these topics. How do you lean into your vulnerability, do you feel able to express how you feel, regularly? Consider having a non-judgemental discussion about the impact of the myth on you and your partner.

True equality requires more than just acknowledging the problem. It demands action.

Pause and Reflect

Reflect on this chapter. How has it made you feel? What change in your life could you make as a result of reading this chapter? What help do you need to minimise the impact of emotional labour and the 2nd shift in your life?

Reflect on the areas where you feel unsupported, whether in your relationships, workplace, or community. What's keeping you trapped? What specific changes or resources would make the greatest difference for your well-being?

What steps can you take to become an advocate for equality and inclusion in your personal life or workplace? How might this shift not only your experience but also contribute to support for others?

'You can't do it all. No one can have two full-time jobs, have perfect children, and cook three meals and be multi-orgasmic until dawn... Superwoman is the adversary of the women's movement'.
— *Gloria Steinem*

Living the Myth

Part Two

Chapter Four
The Weight of Guilt and Shame

Guilt and shame are two emotions so deeply intertwined in the lives of modern women that they often blur into one, especially in the exhausting pursuit of 'having it all' while grappling with the reality of doing it all. These feelings creep up when we finally pause, even if just for a breath, even in our dreams.

As Brené Brown explains in her *Listening to Shame* Ted Talk,[lxxii] 'shame is organised by gender. For men it's "don't be perceived as weak." For women it's "do it all, do it perfectly and never flap." Shame for women is a web of unattainable conflicting messages of who we are supposed to be.'

In a 2022 study,[lxxiii] women listed more reasons than men to feel guilty when considering their personal and professional lives, with women feeling more parental and family guilt. This is endearingly labelled the 'Guilt Gap'. Sure, men feel guilt, but it seems women have a habit of feeling guiltier in more areas of their life.

But guilt and shame are more than just emotions. They are social and psychological forces that keep us chasing a shifting ideal, overburdened, and in a perpetual state of self-criticism. When we peel back the layers of guilt and shame, we see that they're deeply rooted in the myths, pressures, and unworkable standards that women are expected to meet.

We hear a near-constant cacophony of mixed messages, whispering that no matter what we do, it's never enough. We feel guilty because we missed a school play, couldn't attend a team night out, had to leave work at the stated time (our contracted hours), don't want to have sex (or do want to have sex), or forget to respond to the friend or family member who needs us. Shame takes over and transforms that into 'I am a bad person'.

Let's think about it in the context of hyper sexualisation, we're guilted into not having the perfect bodies and shamed into believing it's our fault when we are sexually assaulted. When it comes to motherhood, we're guilted into buying the latest 'things' for our kids and shamed for being absent while working to afford them.

While guilt and shame often go together, they are different in important ways. Guilt is typically associated with specific actions or behaviours. It's the feeling we get when we believe we've done something wrong or fallen short in some way. I didn't spend enough time with my kids/partner/friends/parents today. I didn't go to the gym. I didn't finish that project at work on time. I didn't complete my to-do list. Guilt tells us that we've failed to meet an expectation or standard.

Shame, on the other hand, goes deeper. Shame is about who we are. Shame attacks our sense of self-worth, turning perceived failures into evidence that we are fundamentally flawed, it spirals us downwards leading to self-loathing.

The myth of 'having it all, doing it all and being it all' and the constant attack from social media is the perfect breeding ground for both guilt and shame. The never-ending pursuit of this ideal means that we're always falling short somewhere. And when we do, guilt tells us we're not working hard enough, while shame tells us we're just not enough as people.

The power of shame lies in its ability to silence us, to make us feel unworthy, and to prevent us from reaching our full potential. Shame doesn't just make us feel bad, it corrodes our sense of identity and self-worth. For women, who are conditioned to believe they must excel in every role, mother, partner, professional, friend - shame becomes a crippling force that holds us back.

Here's how shame negatively impacts women:

Self-Sabotage: Shame can lead to self-sabotaging behaviours. When we feel unworthy or inadequate, we may hold ourselves back from pursuing opportunities or taking risks. Shame tells us we're not capable or deserving, so we don't even try. We fear judgment or failure, so we avoid situations that could potentially highlight our perceived flaws.

Perfectionism & People-Pleasing: Shame often fuels perfectionism and people-pleasing. The belief that we are not good enough leads us to overcompensate by striving for impossible standards and not setting boundaries. Both are coping mechanisms, a way to shield ourselves from the feelings of inadequacy.

Isolation: Shame thrives in secrecy. It isolates us, making us feel like we're alone in our struggles. We don't want to admit our feelings, so we hide them, creating a barrier between ourselves and others.

Erosion of Self-Worth: Over time, shame erodes our self-esteem and self-worth. It can lead to a cycle of negative thinking, where we start to believe we're inherently flawed. This can affect every area of our lives, from our personal relationships to our careers.

Carys, a 36-year-old mother of two children under five, shares her struggles with balancing work and family life. Before becoming a mother, she was a full-time Marketing Director. She recently opted for a part-time role, working as a client director, finishing each day at 2:30 PM.

Despite her gratitude for the flexibility, Carys finds herself overwhelmed by guilt and shame. 'I feel guilty if I can't drop my children to school, and I feel guilty because I now work part-time. I am not working as many hours as I had to hand work to colleagues to finish,' she explains. Her current role remains demanding, and she constantly transitions between her professional responsibilities and motherhood throughout the week. 'The guilt is overwhelming at times. I feel I am not accomplishing anything well,' Carys admits.

With no support network nearby, she and her partner, Ollie, face additional challenges. Carys reflects: 'I do feel the pressure to return to working full-time. I feel shame that I can't contribute as much financially at home, and I feel shame when I can't take on additional work to support my workplace. I have to set stringent boundaries, and I've realised I am not "producing" as much as I used to when I was full-time, and there is never any time for me.'

The myth of 'having it all' plays directly into the toxic, perfectionist, overachievement culture that tells us our worth is based on how much we can produce and how perfectly we can perform. We're expected to manage demanding careers, be devoted mothers, maintain healthy relationships, stay fit and healthy, be a perfect daughter and sibling, all whilst making it look effortless.

Then we're often caught in an endless battle and when we feel guilty for not maintaining any one of those standards, we eat shame for breakfast, lunch and dinner, because we're told we are the problem, as other women seem to manage all this effortlessly - so just try harder.

Men struggle with shame and guilt in different ways. Men can experience 'provider guilt', conditioned to see financial success and career achievement as their primary value. If they struggle financially, lose a job or fail to provide in the way they believe they should, guilt creeps in - even when external factors are to blame. Many fathers, especially those raised in households where their own fathers were distant, may feel guilty if they are aware they repeat the same patterns and they may feel guilty for being unable to emotionally connect.

Shame is one of the most powerful yet under discussed emotions for men. It lurks beneath the surface, shaping behaviour, relationships and self-worth, often in ways men themselves don't fully recognise. In a similar way to women, it tells men they are not enough.

Early conditioning teaches boys to reject vulnerability and embrace self-sufficiency. Messages like 'man-up', or 'boys don't cry' create a rigid framework where any display of emotion is perceived as failure. This early conditioning creates a 'shame core' - making men feel they must always be in control and perform at a high level in all areas of their life.

To break the cycle of guilt and shame, we need to approach these emotions from a psychological standpoint. The key is to recognise them for what they are, socially conditioned responses, and to challenge the myths and beliefs that keep us trapped in this cycle. Below are some strategies that can help.

The first step in overcoming guilt and shame is recognising that these emotions are not innate, they are learned. Much of the guilt and shame we experience comes from external societal pressures, not from our own internal values.

Shame thrives on self-criticism. The more we beat ourselves up for not being good enough, the more power shame has over us. The antidote to shame is self-compassion, treating ourselves with the same kindness and understanding that we would offer to a friend. When you feel guilt or shame creeping in, ask yourself: What would I say to a friend in this situation? Then, apply that same kindness to yourself.

When we open up about our struggles, we create connection and dissolve guilt and shame's power. Talk to trusted friends, mentors, or even a therapist about the guilt and shame you're experiencing. You'll likely discover that you're not alone in these feelings, and that can be healing.

Redefine what success looks like for you. The myth of 'having it all' is a societal construct designed to keep women feeling inadequate, as perpetual consumers instead of economic change agents. True success isn't about doing everything perfectly; it's about living in alignment with your own values. Take time to reflect on what truly matters to you and let go of the pressures to meet someone else's definition of success.

In our research, we observed many women experiencing both guilt and shame in their work and personal lives inevitably led them to do more and more and burn out. Interestingly some of the women we interviewed had transitioned past this pressure, having established boundaries and priorities. They were clear about their own values and life principles.

Renaye Edwards' story weaves a complex narrative of work-life balance, serving as a beacon of resilience and innovation in the contemporary business landscape. As the co-founder of Digital Radish, she embarked on her entrepreneurial journey driven not only by professional ambitions but also by a deeper quest for meaning and legacy.

Her story transitions from that of a career-focused individual to a mother striving for balance, highlighting the profound complexities women encounter in leadership roles. Our interview revealed the multifaceted challenges and triumphs of navigating personal and professional realms, offering insights into the persistent pursuit of fulfillment and equilibrium.

Renaye's story begins with an introspective reflection on her early career, marked by achievements yet shadowed by an unfulfilled desire for a more significant impact. The inception of Digital Radish was a leap towards filling this void, driven by a vision to craft a legacy beyond conventional corporate accolades. Her narrative takes a pivotal turn with her transition into motherhood, introducing her to the multifaceted challenges of balancing professional aspirations with personal commitments.

A candid recount of the postpartum phase shows the stark realities of returning to work, navigating the emotional turmoil of separation from her newborn. This period epitomised the struggle of countless women torn between career progression and familial bonds. Despite these challenges, Renaye's entrepreneurial path afforded her the flexibility to mold her schedule around her daughter's needs, a testament to the advantages of leadership in crafting a work-life harmony.

Still, she confronts the ideal of 'having it all', a construct that often leaves women grappling with guilt and the fear of inadequacy. She challenges this notion, advocating for a pragmatic approach to balance, emphasising the importance of setting realistic expectations and boundaries.

Renaye sheds light on the disproportionate burden of emotional labour borne by women, exacerbated by societal expectations and traditional gender roles. Her experience highlights the critical role of supportive partnerships and networks in mitigating these pressures, enabling women to pursue their ambitions without forsaking their personal lives.

She offers sage advice to women navigating similar paths. Emphasising the significance of self-compassion, the courage to define personal success beyond societal benchmarks, and the importance of cherishing meaningful relationships over professional achievements. Renaye's insights culminate in a powerful call to action for systemic change, advocating for policies and cultural shifts that support women's aspirations both in the workplace and at home.

Renaye's journey encapsulates the intricacies, hurdles, and opportunities for fulfillment inherent in the quest for work-life balance. Her narrative, deeply integrated into our discussion, acts as a reflection of the realities confronted by women in leadership roles as well as a source of inspiration and direction for those seeking a harmonious and meaningful existence. Through her experiences, we explore the delicate dance between professional ambition and personal well-being, offering insights and strategies for navigating these dual demands with grace and resilience.

Remember you are enough.

Letting go of the myth of 'having it all' and the reality of 'doing it all' means accepting that we can't do everything, and that's okay. We don't need to be perfect mothers, flawless professionals, or always-present friends. We can be imperfect, human, and still worthy of love, success, and happiness.

As Dr. Clarissa Pinkola Estés writes in her seminal work, *Women Who Run with the Wolves*: 'I've seen women insist on cleaning everything in the house before they could sit down to write… and you know, it's a funny thing about housecleaning… it never comes to an end. Perfect way to stop a woman. A woman must be careful not to allow over-responsibility to steal her necessary creative rest, riffs, and raptures. She simply must put her foot down and say no to half of what she believes she "should" be doing'.

We need to harness strong self-awareness, define our own values and life principles as well as share our stories consistently so we are not living in the shadows of shame or guilt.

Notes for Male Allies

Shame is a tough emotion to manage, particularly with some of the topics explored in this book. It is critical you understand how shame or guilt may impact your response to certain subjects. It is hard to listen to discussions about gender-based violence, for example. Help to break the cycle by becoming emotionally connected.

Here is how shame can manifest for men: Anger and Aggression; Perfectionism and Overachievement; Emotional Withdrawal; Addiction and Risk-Taking Behaviour Fear of Intimacy. Breaking free from the shame cycle requires work - redefining masculinity, creating a version that embraces emotional strength, self-awareness and authenticity.

Pause and Reflect

How has the pursuit of perfection and the glorification of busyness shaped your sense of self-worth? What would it feel like to release yourself from these expectations?

When you experience guilt or shame for not meeting certain standards, what stories are you telling yourself? How can you rewrite these narratives with self-compassion at the center?

To overcome shame: Identify your shame triggers - where do you feel like you are failing? Ask yourself if you created this standard or was it placed on me? Practise self-compassion and reach for your inner ally or coach. Shame is loud, so compassion has to be even louder.

'Talk to yourself like you would to someone you love'.
— Brené Brown

Chapter Five
Building

Writing this book has meant asking tough questions of ourselves. One of them is how we can change society and culture for our daughters? Is the myth of 'having it all' empowerment, entrapment or a business model?

Sam shares her observations from mentoring and coaching young women: 'There is nothing wrong with ambition, aspiration and drive, but underneath this, I saw a real fear of missing out, comparison, and not achieving enough - quickly enough - or being held back by a fear of being judged online'.

She continues: 'These young women would throw themselves into overwork based on the advice of mentors taking on additional projects to gain "visibility" and land the next promotion. Inevitably, they would plateau, throttled back by an HR bell curve. This would cause them to work harder, without adequate reward. Equally, the women who chose to have children would become frustrated with themselves for feeling like they couldn't be as productive as before when, in fact, they were taking on the equivalent of two full-time roles, recovering from childbirth and still rocking it.'

Sam adds: 'It's worth noting I hear a lot of younger women questioning their leadership aspiration when they finally get into the workplace. Very often, they see senior women overworking, whilst trying to juggle childcare responsibilities, and Gen Z women are actively debating whether this is what they want.'

Research by Thomas Curran and Andrew Hill[lxxiv] shows that perfectionism, particularly self-oriented perfectionism is increasing amongst young people, compelling them to compete relentlessly in the name of meritocracy while facing raised expectations from demanding parents.

In *Never Enough: When Achievement Culture Becomes Toxic – and What We Can Do About It*, Jennifer Breheny Wallace critiques toxic achievement culture, where societal pressures normalise overwork, hyper-competition, and burnout as prerequisites for success. This culture elevates grades, awards, social status, and perfection over personal growth, fulfilment, and well-being, driving youth, particularly young women, into cycles of anxiety and inadequacy.

Similarly, Byung-Chul Han, in *The Burnout Society*, explores the societal 'imperative to achieve', which reduces individuals to 'performance machines' and leaves them disconnected from the present moment, self-worth, and mental well-being. Han describes this as a 'crisis of satisfaction', the incessant pursuit of future goals strips individuals of contentment and deep reflection. Together, these perspectives show how the hyper-achievement narrative, endemic in modern society, not only undermines mental health but also disproportionately affects young women who are feel pressured to excel in all facets of life.

The myth drives young women into overwork, perfectionism, people pleasing and scarcity mindset, the cornerstones of wounded feminine. It conditions women to believe their worth is measured by relentless achievement, pushing them into cycles of fear-based decision making. Left unchecked it can keep young women stuck in underpaid roles, toxic workplaces and harmful relationships.

Instead of thriving, they remain in survival mode, unable to progress toward self-actualisation - the highest level of Maslow's Hierarchy of Needs, where fulfilment and purpose reside. Basic needs such as rest, health and safety are neglected, replaced by the constant pressure to do more, be more and prove more.

From an early age, this myth is ingrained in young women: 'Have it all. Never enough. Achieve at all costs.' By the time a girl turns 16, she has already seen over 200,000+ images telling her what beauty is and isn't. Social media amplifies this conditioning, feeding a culture of comparison and external validation where self-worth is measured in fleeting likes and followers. Research shared in Forbes Magazine [lxxv] confirms social media use negatively impacts young women's mental health, reinforcing feelings of inadequacy and not belonging. At its worst it fuels competition between women at a time when we need to collaborate.

As our young women face into an increasingly volatile, uncertain, complex and ambiguous future, they are often told to be more resilient. This term is habitually weaponised in the western world. While resilience is an essential skill, it is often misused to shift responsibility away from dysfunctional workplaces and societies.

Women are told to 'be resilient' in the face of toxic managers, bullying, impossible workloads and structural discrimination, where the load of navigating unjust systems is placed solely onto the individual rather than creating systemic change.

Although resilience is important, it should never be a badge of honour for enduring suffering. Humans are not designed to be in a perpetual state of adaptation and endurance. There are health costs that come with over-resilience, such as an over-active nervous system, causing chronic stress. Being resilient should never come at the expense of your well-being. The strongest form of self-trust is the ability to recognise when to persist and when to leave.

We know our young women need to be equipped to compete in today's climate, but they must do so from a place of choice, wholeness, balance, and purpose. Equally important, we need to ensure that the system is set up to enable them to succeed.

Starting out - Am I good enough?
At just 17 years old, Scarlett is finishing her final term at a prestigious drama school in London, carving her path toward a lifelong dream she's been pursuing since she became a professional actor at 11. Clear-eyed and full of determination, Scarlett radiates a wisdom and resilience far beyond her years. But even with her drive and accomplishments, she's no stranger to the pressures young women face, particularly in a highly competitive industry like acting.

'I often don't feel good enough,' she admits. 'At drama school, it can be really hard not to compare yourself to others. I hold myself to a high standard, and this is especially true in the acting industry, where it's highly competitive for each role. And it's very competitive for girls and young women because there aren't lots of boys or young men in the industry, and they tend to be prioritised for places in schools. So, I feel as a young woman, I've had to do so much more and prove myself more, and that really contributes to not feeling good enough.'

Growing up, Scarlett faced the common teenage pressures of 'fitting in'. Over time, though, she has embraced her individuality and found her own unique style. The pressure, however, hasn't disappeared entirely. 'It's simply shifted. There's lots of pressure,' she says. 'I feel like I constantly need to be doing something to achieve something. At 16, it was the pressure to get good grades; now it's the pressure of getting into a good drama school.'

Despite this, Scarlett's bubbly personality shines through, especially when she reflects on what truly matters to her. 'I've realised the power of learning through life experiences and slowing down to enjoy life,' she shares.

'I want to spend my life doing something I love. I think wealth comes from doing what you love. Obviously, money is important, but there's more to life than that... like happiness.'

Scarlett has thoughtfully considered the roles women play in society, shaped by what she's seen in her own family. 'In my family, I've watched my mum doing the majority of the work at home and working really hard outside of the home.' She quips: 'That's not for me! I think it needs to be a better partnership, equal 50/50 in the home. Otherwise, that's not fair on the mum or woman.'

When asked about how she defines success, Scarlett's reflections are inspiring. 'When I was younger, I was very focused on what other people were doing and worrying about what they thought. Now, I think success is about having fun and friendships. My friendships bring me so much joy,' she says. However, like many her age, she does worry about her future and finding fulfilment in her career. 'My fears are mainly around being stuck doing a job for years that I don't enjoy, that feels mundane and routine.'

Scarlett's perspective is refreshingly positive, especially as she laughs about the urgency society often places on achieving success by a certain age. 'There always feels like this pressure

- you can do better - and I do feel the pressure to do so much before I turn 30. But I'm beginning to realise,' she says with a chuckle, 'that life doesn't end when you turn 30!'

Entering the Workforce - The Confidence Gap

Sophie shares her story as a recent graduate from St. Andrew's university in Scotland. She attended an all-girls private school from the age of 11. She has just started her first role at a global consultancy firm and reflects on how positive her educational experience was: 'Growing up, I was told I could do and be anything. When I left school, I basically felt like I could run the world, and that continued throughout my education. I left university feeling confident, but moving into the workforce has been eye-opening, and it's had a pretty big impact on me.'

When asked to give specifics, Sophie mentions a lack of positive support and a constant feeling of inadequacy, as well as being asked to take on more and more responsibilities. 'I have no issue working hard, but there's an expectation that I have to work "extra" to prove myself. I know I have a lot to learn, but I definitely feel anxious a lot of the time. I don't feel the environment is set up for me to succeed. It feels like it's either sink or swim. There seems to be this unspoken rule that we have to experience a tough environment to build our resilience or, as one manager put it, "earn our stripes".'

Building a Career - The Importance of Allyship

Mia is in her early 30s and recently married. She joined a global Pharma firm as an intern and later entered their graduate programme. She was a first-class honours student and as she started her career, she was praised frequently for her brilliance at work.

As she proved herself capable, she was given more and more responsibility, eventually finding herself navigating her role without a manager while leading a business-critical strategy.

Mia aspires to become a leader and was told that gaining sales experience would be crucial for her career. She recalls: 'It was the worst career move I ever made. From the start, I hated it and felt completely ill-equipped. The role didn't align with my strengths, and I was at risk of being placed on a PIP (performance improvement plan).'

As part of her improvement plan, Mia was told to change her appearance along with how she spoke. She revealed how this impacted her self-esteem. To add further insult, she shares: 'I had been without a manager for the previous two years, I was already under-levelled compared to my peers. I was taking on lots of additional projects but faced constant pushback when I asked for salary or level increases. It was demoralising.'

Despite being previously considered a high-potential future leader, Mia found herself stuck until a male leader took her under his wing and sponsored her. 'I was about three months away from leaving the company after three successive quarters of not making my quota,' she says. 'He moved me into his team, and this led to a huge turnaround in my career, he was an exceptional ally and mentor and through him I found a role I loved and flourished in. He also introduced me to several senior women leaders in our company who really supported, mentored and amplified me.'

Reflecting on her journey, Mia offers advice to younger women: 'You need to use your voice and ask for support. It can feel scary and daunting, especially if, like me, you tend to people-please. Take the time to evaluate your career path; it is easy to take on a role when people tell you that you "should" do something. Critically reflect on what the role will give you and whether it plays to your strengths and skills, it's also ok to move sideways to gain experience.'

She concludes: 'And it's ok to fail, failure provides crucial insights if we learn to apply the lessons to our lives in thoughtful ways.'

Forging a New Direction - Build Success on Your Terms
Leanne Maskell, best-selling author of four books, is an activist founder of ADHD Works and ex-Vogue model. Leanne shares her story growing up as a young model and offers a deeply personal perspective on how the 'myth of having it all' has shaped her life. At 13 years old, she was a professional model, being held up as an icon of perfection.
'I probably looked like I had it all. I was in Vogue magazine portrayed as a woman, being used to model to other women what they should look like, even though I was a child,' she continues: 'I did well at school, but I've always felt very much that I am not enough.'

Leanne went on to study law at university - not because she loved it, just because, 'I had no idea what else to do, and society says, "That's a good job". I soon realised studying subjects we don't really like means we take jobs we don't really want; to make and spend money so we can feel better about ourselves.'

Despite all the external trappings of success, the burden of meeting society's standards had a significant impact on Leanne's mental health resulting in a 5-year mental health crisis. Her ADHD diagnosis freed her a little from trying to meet some of those expectations. Looking back, Leanne reflects that the myth of having it all affected her a lot, feeling the pressure of having to meet certain standards and the realisation that it's impossible.

Now, Leanne is making her own life, as a successful author and entrepreneur, although as she states she struggles with the pressures of her personal and professional life as a woman with AuDHD (Autistic & ADHD - Leanne was diagnosed with autism in 2024). She shares: 'On the outside, I look like I am doing well from society's perspective because I run a company, I appear on TV and the radio, but underneath this, no one would realise that I often feel suicidal.'

When asked about how she now defines success she adds: 'Success is doing what you want; now I very much try to live my life based on what my version of success looks like for me, which is being happy, being able to do the things you want to do and not feeling like you need to do more, it's very freeing.'

When asked what advice she would give to young women, Leanne shares her wisdom: 'Go and create something you want and put it out in the world in the way that works for you. You definitely don't have to pick one job and purpose in life, - live your life and enjoy your time here.'

She ends: 'Oh, and get off social media. I know it's really hard, apps take over your life and before you know it the algorithms shape your life and who you are as a person, and it can be really hard to find out who you truly are.'

Farah concludes: 'Is it really too much to ask that systems and society support our young women? We've made this a woman's issue - but it's not. Toxic achievement culture, scarcity mindset, overwork, and the myth of 'having it all' are not personal failings; they are systemic problems, rooted in hyper-consumerism and patriarchal structures. For too long, society has gaslit women into believing this is their problem to solve.'

She argues: 'We must stop perpetuating this myth for the generations to come. We need to hold those in power accountable and not just advocate for change but demand it. We must build societies that meet the needs of our young women, so they thrive. If we don't challenge these structures now, we are complicit in the cycle we claim to fight against.'

Both Sam and Farah agree that young women should treat their career as a marathon, not a sprint. Most Millennial, Gen Z and Alpha women will be in the workforce for at least 50 years of their life. Their advice is to plan for longevity and build a network that can support your career, research shows an inner circle of close female associates helps women to advance to senior positions. Allies and sponsors will help too, but don't neglect the sisterhood.

Building Strong Foundations – The Antidote to the Myth
Breaking free from the myth requires more than just rejecting unrealistic expectations. Sam believes now is the time to cultivate strong psychological and emotional foundations alongside academic studies. Sam observes: 'So many studies show girls are more likely to struggle with self-doubt, perfectionism and a fear of failure compared to boys. I have mentored a lot of young women, and I see those coming through the UK state school system as particularly at risk. With the ongoing mental health crises - these subjects need to be on an equal footing with STEM and ARTS.

She continues: 'The world needs to prioritise mental well-being and sustainable ambition over relentless productivity. This means creating spaces where everyone can rest without guilt, embrace imperfections without shame and define their version of success.'

Sam concludes: 'the antidote to the myth isn't doing more, it's doing what matters.'

The future we want for our daughters requires more than dismantling old myths, it demands we build something new. True success is not a checklist of achievements, but a life rooted in authenticity, self-trust, and purpose. If we want lasting change, we must shift the focus from what young women should accomplish to who they can become, giving them the freedom to craft lives that are whole, purposeful and meaningful. But this transformation is not just about empowering daughters; it's about raising sons who value and respect equality. As mothers, mentors, and leaders, women play a critical role in shaping the attitudes of the next generation, ensuring that our sons grow into men who see women as equals and partners in every sphere of life.

Our career building steps to success

- **Set short-term goals that drive action.** Long-term goals (3–5 years) can feel distant. Start with 6-month and 1-year targets focused on experiences, finances, learning, and self-development. Small wins create momentum.
- **Watch your mindset.** Thoughts become Feelings become Actions become Results. Manage negativity and scarcity thoughts, remember the algorithms feed you based on what you scroll through.
- **Stay flexible - careers aren't linear.** Think of it like a game of 'snakes and ladders'. Adaptability shortens your path to success. Unexpected turns can be opportunities.
- **Use the 3x3 career plan.** Break your career into three phases: early, mid, and senior/exiting. Evaluate opportunities against three criteria: Does it align with your purpose? Does it offer experience, responsibility, or development? Does it increase your wealth or

happiness? Not every move will tick all three boxes. Aim for at least two.

- **Redefine success on your terms.** Growth comes from both wins and failures. Stop comparing your path to friends or family expectations. Own your version of success.
- **Take on high-value projects and negotiate your worth.** Side hustles, big projects, and leadership opportunities can accelerate your career, if they serve you. Avoid 'cast-off' tasks with little return and always advocate for fair compensation.
- **Set boundaries - overwork is not a badge of honour.** Know your worth and protect your time. Chasing toxic achievement won't serve you long-term. Self-trust is your best asset.
- **Master storytelling – it is a power tool.** Great communicators get noticed. Whether pitching ideas, leading teams, or networking, compelling storytelling is a game-changer.
- **Understand people – it is the ultimate skill.** Human behaviour shapes every workplace and opportunity. The more you understand it, the better outcomes you will achieve.
- **Don't forget human connection.** We are social beings and need human connection, find ways to engage with other people if you work remotely all the time

A Note for Male Allies

Men play a critical role in advancing gender equality by actively supporting early in career women. Active mentoring, sponsorship, amplifying women's contributions and challenging discrimination when it happens are all important facets of strong allyship. Be aware of the discrimination young women can face and observe your own biases.

Supporting Early in Career Men

As we outlined earlier, many young men are struggling and feel adrift, caught between dated ideals of masculinity and the reality of modern workplaces and homes that demand more from them. It is vital we bring our young men on the journey with us and support them and let them know they are equally welcome, encourage to embrace authentic masculinity and understand and acknowledge wounded masculinity. Mentoring, sponsorship are all vital parts of this. Research suggests male employees with female mentors report greater career satisfaction and are more likely to champion gender equality themselves.

Pause and Reflect

Reflect on how the messages you received in your own upbringing about achievement and success have shaped your beliefs today. How might these beliefs influence the way you support and guide young women in your life?

When you find yourself caught in scarcity thinking or focusing on what's lacking, what small shifts, like gratitude or self-compassion might help you reframe your perspective?

Imagine the strongest foundation you could build for your life: one grounded in your values, purpose, and authentic self. What steps can you take to nurture this foundation and let it guide your ambitions?

'I raise up my voice - not so that I can shout,
but so that those without a voice can be heard.
We cannot all succeed when half of us are held back'.
- Malala Yousafzai

Chapter Six
Balancing

One morning just outside London, Sam and Farah met up, and together they explored their shared experiences of navigating womanhood, motherhood, and careers, while wrestling with the myth of 'having it all'. That day, the idea for this book took root. This chapter is devoted to the stories of women we interviewed. We hope you recognise your own story and realise you are not alone.

A quick search on 'work/life balance for women' yields millions of articles, books, blogs, academic studies, and podcasts. In recent years, Sheryl Sandberg's book *Lean In* served as a manifesto for female empowerment, inspiring the creation of 'Lean In Circles' around the globe. Through these movements, celebrity and industry role models have championed messages of personal empowerment. That balancing it all is simply a matter of mindset, resilience and individual effort - encouraging women to 'fix' themselves as a response to structural inequalities.

This brand of neoliberal feminism blends seamlessly with consumerism, marketing empowerment as another thing for women to pay for rather than a birthright or something that requires systemic change. While personal agency is undeniably important, and we are all for empowered women taking ownership of their destiny, this narrative conveniently shifts responsibility from organisations and governments onto women. We do not believe empowerment should be a solo endeavour.

In *Happiness and the Liberal Imagination: How Superwoman Became Balanced*, Catherine Rottenberg [lxxvi] argues that neoliberal feminism has shifted from a focus on equality to one on balance and happiness, particularly for women who juggle multiple roles. Although the 'balanced woman' narrative may seem more attainable than the 'Superwoman' ideal, it again places the burden of achieving work-life balance solely on women. Instead of advocating for systemic change, it compels women to excel professionally while managing traditional roles at home, all in pursuit of becoming the ultimate form of human capital.

This unforgiving pressure to perform in all spheres ignores a fundamental truth: Women's lives are not static. They are shaped by transitions, seasons and evolving identities. Furthermore, the notion of balance assumes all aspects of a woman's identity are acknowledged and equally valued by society, yet we know that is not the case, professional achievements are hard won, and caregiving or personal well-being are either taken for granted or actively penalised.

Nowhere is this more evident than in motherhood, a shift so immense it has been compared to adolescence in its intensity. It even has its own beautiful name - *matrescence* - capturing the profound psychological, emotional, and physical transformation of motherhood.

Whereas adolescence is widely recognised and accommodated as a critical period of development, matrescence or motherhood remains undervalued and often ignored. Women are left to navigate its challenges alone, whilst being pressured to bounce back into pre-motherhood clothing, productivity and accessibility.

This devaluation reveals the struggle for balance is not simply about managing time more effectively, it's about whose roles and identities are seen as valuable. As long as caregiving remains invisible in economic and workplace structures, balance will remain out of reach for all women.

Recognising matrescence as a distinct and valid phase could offer women a sense of relief, providing the space to redefine success and themselves as they wish. As a society, we must do more to encourage new mothers to share these experiences openly, rather than conforming to picture-perfect ideals portrayed on social media. Just as we allow adolescents to navigate the complexities of their transition, we must also allow mothers the freedom to process their own journey. By doing so, we can begin to normalise these experiences and perhaps reduce the prevalence of postpartum depression, guilt and shame.

In discussing this, it is impossible to ignore the often-contentious topic of maternity leave benefit. Over half of the women we spoke with expressed a desire for a minimum of 12 months of fully paid maternity leave.

Maternity leave laws vary greatly worldwide, shaped by economic conditions, cultural expectations, and government policies. One respondent remarked on the stark difference in maternity benefits outside the large corporation she used to work for, a factor that influenced her decision to remain childfree, as she couldn't justify having a child only to spend her income on childcare.

For example, the United States stands out for its lack of federally mandated paid maternity leave, while Canada offers 15 weeks of maternity leave with an option for parental leave of up to 69 weeks. In the UK, mothers are entitled to 52 weeks of leave though pay levels vary unless employers choose to supplement statutory pay, eligibility criteria must also be met, such as time in employment.

The Nordic countries, however, set a global standard with generous parental leave policies that allow both parents to share up to 16 months of leave. Studies consistently show that extended maternity leave is linked to better health outcomes for both mothers and their babies.

Interestingly, as parental leave becomes more widely available, men are beginning to encounter discrimination for taking extended time off, their desire to spend time with their family in direct opposition to gender norms. Over the past 20 years, the number of countries with legally mandated paternity leave has more than doubled. Yet, the proportion of men who take more than a few days off after their child is born remains small.

These fears often deter men from fully utilising their paternity leave, despite growing evidence that shared parental leave has numerous benefits for family dynamics and child development.[lxxvii]

In our survey, 81% of respondents had children, and nearly half of those with school-age children reported constantly juggling responsibilities without sufficient support. Many relied on pre- or after-school programmes to provide care for their children. For these women, balancing work and family life often comes down to sheer grit, resourcefulness, and determination - the kind of desirable skills needed at the helm of organisations and governments.

One respondent, who works in corporate America as an operations manager, shared her experience of being required to attend 6am meetings every morning for 3 weeks as the business shifted direction. With a baby and toddler at home, the expectation felt impossible: 'I was literally changing diapers on these calls; it felt like such an intrusion.' Her manager, a new father himself, had a different reality. 'He had a stay-at-home wife who was able to look after their baby. I didn't have that luxury. My partner leaves at 5.30 am every morning to get to the city. No one even asked if I could make this work; the assumption was that I would prioritise my work over my caregiving responsibilities.'

She noted that 80% of the people on the call were fathers, yet their default was that their wives would lean in at home while they prioritised work. 'It was such a clear example of privilege and conditioning.'

Our UK based respondents cited the prohibitive cost of childcare, currently ranked as one of the highest in the world. An overwhelming majority expressed a clear demand for free childcare.

Our findings also suggest evolving family dynamics, with several mentions of stay-at-home fathers and a shift in traditional gender roles. This shift hints at potential growing awareness of shared parental responsibilities in modern households, as families reimagine and renegotiate their roles. Interestingly, two paths emerge with this dynamic; a woman able to get ahead and fulfil her career destiny, because the roles have completely reversed; and a woman who holds onto the guilt of not being able to do it all, and overcompensates by overworking at home, despite a stay at home partner.

When we looked at the working patterns of the women in our survey, we found that only 11% worked part-time or on a four-day schedule. Of those working full-time in offices, 62% benefited from a hybrid model that offered some flexibility. However, as we write, numerous large organisations are issuing return-to-office mandates, requiring full-time in-office attendance. This shift will likely intensify pressures on working mothers who already face significant challenges in managing career and family life.

Many women (50.1%)[lxxviii] are now delaying parenthood, with the average age for a first child in the UK now at 30.7 years. As a result, career peaks often coincide with the critical periods of a child's life, such as the demanding school years. Senior roles frequently come with increased travel, evening events, and other obligations that pull parents away from home, just as their children need support with homework, mental health, exams, and university applications. Yet, most parenthood policies remain focused on the early years, leaving many families without adequate support during these later stages.

The current global cost of living crisis creates an economic challenge. For women who want to have a family, their ability to have it as part of their 'all' is severely impacted by rising living expenses, the cost of housing, energy, food and childcare (particularly in the UK). According to MaternityAction.org,[lxxix] families are having to choose whether to have a child at all, and women who have children are having to decide whether to return to work, further impacting their financial stability.

In 2012, Anne-Marie Slaughter, the first woman to serve as Director of Policy Planning at the U.S. State Department, wrote a groundbreaking op-ed for *The Atlantic* titled 'Why Women Still Can't Have It All'.[lxxx] In it, she explored the challenges of juggling a demanding, high-profile role in public office while being a mother to two teenagers. During a public lecture at Oxford, Slaughter offered candid reflections on how unexpectedly difficult it was to fulfil the demands of a government role while also being present for her children at a time when they needed her most.

Slaughter, like many of us, believes that it is possible for both women and men to 'have it all' but not within the constraints of our current economic and societal structures. She pointed out that until we reconfigure the ways our workplaces and societal norms are structured, true balance will remain elusive for many. Her reflections stress the need for systemic change to support parents in pursuing fulfilling careers without sacrificing their roles at home.[lxxxi]

Slaughter's op-ed sparked a wide range of opinions, but it particularly resonated with younger readers who appreciated her vulnerability and honesty. She voiced the struggles of a generation trying to balance ambitious careers with the demands of parenting, a reality that often goes unspoken in public discourse.

Honesty, vulnerability and relatability were referenced in our research when it comes to leadership role models. Women want senior female leaders to be vocal about they how they manage their multiple roles, they do not want PR messaging that glosses over the details or paints a rose-tinted picture to support the corporate message. In today's social media world, women can seek out the reality from the influencers and content creators who share their lives online.

Moreover, women want senior leaders to recognise their position of privilege when sharing their stories. As one woman shared, 'I remember asking a leader how she coped with running the lives of her four boys. I am in a similar position and was searching for the magic recipe as she seemed to do it so effortlessly. It transpired all four of her boys aged from 11 - 17 were at boarding school.'

This desire for honesty from senior female leaders stems from the unforgiving pressure that women feel. One question we asked our respondents was: 'Have you felt pressured to have it all, be it all, and do it all in your life'?

Overwhelmingly, the responses conveyed a constant sense of pressure to meet high standards in careers, parenting, and household management.

Phrases like **'all the time'**, **'always'**, and **'every single day'** were common, reflecting just how deeply ingrained this pressure is. For most, the immense stress is driven by both internal and external expectations. While a few respondents have managed to reframe this pressure in a positive light, the majority describe it as profoundly challenging, with negative effects on their well-being. Words such as exhaustion, anxiety stress, frustration, failing, and resentment were frequently used in the answers, a reminder of the pressure women are under.

Sadly, many of the women acknowledged they often felt the need to pretend they supported the myth, especially in their workplace, out of fear they would be judged for not being ambitious enough, another form of pressure and emotional labouring.

For many, dismantling the myth of 'having it all' feels far more empowering than continuing to strive for an impossible standard as both mother and career woman.

As one respondent put it: 'To have it all is a myth, a trap to keep people, especially mothers, running on the hamster wheel. "Having it all" means never feeling good about yourself, always striving to do more, even when more is never enough. It's a toxic mentality designed to trap people. The truth is, we cannot have it all, and if we can, then we can't have it all at the same time.'

And therefore, perhaps it's this redefining of what we want to have, that becomes most important.

The Reality of Returning to Work

Doreen Pernel, Chief Sales Officer for a leading French Cloud computing company, exemplifies the challenges and triumphs of a modern working mother. Before becoming C-Level, Doreen welcomed her first child into the world. Following four months maternity leave, she returned to her beloved and demanding role, armed with a well-thought-out plan to reintegrate into her professional life.

Despite her foresight and career determination, Doreen quickly encountered the complex realities of juggling motherhood and a high-profile career. She confronts a widely held societal belief: 'This notion of women having it all is a myth; in my opinion, it's completely unrealistic. It's impossible to have it all, especially when you are responsible for caring for others. Without support, managing everything is unfeasible.' This bold statement lays the foundation for an open discussion about the complexities of managing career ambitions and family commitments, reflecting the core of Doreen's experiences as a working mother.

In her analysis of the pressures and unrealistic expectations facing working mothers, Doreen shed light on a critical aspect of the conversation: 'There are two types of people. Some will claim they manage everything perfectly, which can make others feel inadequate and guilty.'

She continues: 'On the other hand, you'll find more direct people that will break this myth and even sometimes crack a joke to make it even more enjoyable to share.'

Doreen elaborates, observing that often those who appear to 'have it all' are either bolstered by a robust support network or are in a strong financial position that allows them to afford additional help, such as nannies and housekeepers.

This reality brings into focus the often-unspoken disparity in the experiences of working mothers, challenging the myth of effortless perfection and underscoring the significant role that resources and support play in shaping these experiences.

Sharing insights from her own life, Doreen spoke about her return to work following her maternity leave: 'Returning to work after maternity leave is a different experience. The working days are not the same as they used to be.' This comment stresses the significant readjustment that accompanies a return to professional life post-childbirth.

Speaking candidly about workplace attitudes towards parenting, Doreen stated: 'Parenting can be challenging, especially if you feel alone in this situation and you are going through a sleep deprivation phase. I try my best to create a safe environment for my team and peers to share and seek help from each other to break the loneliness circle.' This frank admission brings to light the often-hidden struggles of working parents.

On the crucial aspect of support systems, she remarked, 'We rely on our families. This familial support is integral to our approach in balancing work and family life with my partner.' Doreen's acknowledgement of her support network emphasises its vital role in navigating the demands of her dual roles.

Regarding the division of household responsibilities, Doreen articulated: 'My partner and I decided early on to divide each household task between each other from childcare to groceries. We both contribute evenly and found our balance this way.' This division of labour within her household is a great illustration of the importance of partnership and communication when sharing domestic responsibilities.

Doreen went on to highlight the importance of strategic planning and communication: 'If you have the opportunity to plan your pregnancy, do it meticulously with your partner, family, friends, and workplace. Preparing for the phases before, during, and after maternity leave is critical.'

One of the best pieces of advice she had while pregnant was to plan everything before leaving the workplace for her teams and most importantly having an organised plan for returning to work, from scheduling, projects, events and even a folder of 'must reads' that her leaders reporting to her would have had ready for her.

Challenging Traditional Parenting Roles

Simone Larsson is an AI Expert and Evangelist Focused on Responsibility & Ethics & founder of The Good Tech Company. In her candid narrative, she shares her journey of navigating motherhood and career, highlighting the deep-rooted values instilled by her parents. Born and raised in the Caribbean, she was influenced by her father's emphasis on education and her mother's drive for independence. Her mother, having grown up seeing her own mother dependent on a husband for financial support, was determined to chart a different course.

After leaving her previous employer, Simone started her consultancy, only to discover she was pregnant shortly after. Her journey to motherhood was marked by challenges, including the spectre of previous miscarriages. The experience of navigating pregnancy and work without structured maternity leave led her to consciously design the life she wanted, avoiding the pressure to conform to traditional work norms.

She discusses the cultural nuances and expectations around parenting roles, noting the striking differences in attitudes towards fathers versus mothers in child-rearing and household responsibilities. Her Swedish husband's hands-on approach to parenting and willingness to pause his career to care for their child contrasts sharply with societal norms in other cultures.

Simone acknowledges the ongoing struggle to balance professional commitments with the desire to be present for her child. She points out the challenges of managing emotional labour and the often-unequal distribution of household responsibilities, even in a supportive partnership.

Our interview delves into the complexities of navigating motherhood and career, highlighting the need for more equitable sharing of parenting and domestic duties and greater societal understanding of the unique challenges faced by working mothers.

Simone emphasises the importance of self-awareness and conscious decision-making in life, particularly in choosing a partner and in shaping one's personal and professional journey. She advocates for open discussions in relationships to address and balance the distribution of emotional and household labour. Her story reflects the broader challenges faced by many working mothers, seeking to balance their careers with their roles as parents and partners.

Childfree by choice, can I have it all?

Efe is 42, and an IT Director in the UK's National Health Service, she is married with 2 dogs and was always clear about her decision not to have children.

Efe is used to explaining her rationale to well-meaning family and she explains that her decision was frowned upon in her culture. 'I come from a big family and I am the oldest. I spent a lot of my childhood caring for siblings, and watching my mum take on all the care responsibilities and work two jobs. I decided that I didn't want that. I also wanted to go to university - I was the first in my family to go.'

She adds with a wry smile: 'So, instead, I am the cool aunt.' More importantly, Efe shares her deep sense of wanting to make a difference and living a fulfilled life. She states there are more than enough children in the world and that she didn't want to add to that.

When we asked her what the myth meant to her, she shares: 'From my perspective, it's the assumption I must have children to fulfil my destiny. I am often accused of being selfish. Lots of people ask me if it is my choice not to have kids and many people ask me if my partner is happy with the decision. There seems to be a view of childless women that we are incomplete without children.' She continues: 'My mum often asks me who will take care of me when I am old. I have

10 nieces and nephews, plus younger siblings, so I am placing the responsibility firmly on their shoulders,' she says with a laugh.

As Efe reflects on the women she works with, she says: 'I don't know how they manage it. My mum's struggle was tough, and she worked around our school hours as a cleaner. It often seems like so many women are walking a tightrope, and many of them seem unhappy in the juggle.'

Choosing to Stay at Home

Leaving her career as a general counsel for an LA film studio was not an easy decision for Esha. She had worked hard for her salary, stock, benefits, and pension, but after her IVF twins were born prematurely and spent months in the NICU, the thought of daycare felt unbearable. She shares: 'One of my babies was still tube-fed, and with minimal maternity leave, I felt I hadn't had enough time with them, those first few months were so overwhelming.'

A breakdown in a hospital parking lot led her partner to make the decision for them - he would take over financially so she could stay home. Though grateful for his support, Esha admits she struggled with the loss of independence and found it difficult to ask for money. 'I've always worked and earned my own money; it was such a hard pivot, and really impacted my sense of worth.'

Letting go of her career identity was even harder. Esha had internalised the belief that she should be able to "do it all," and when the roles shifted, she overcompensated. She recalls: 'I totally threw myself into proving myself and my value as a new mom and supportive wife. I felt I should do that as I was no longer financially contributing to the household. I think I turned motherhood into a game I had to win at all costs. What no one tells you is that sleep deprivation and caring for two babies make doing it all impossible.'

This pressure became overwhelming, and Esha was diagnosed with postpartum depression, making her feel like even more of a failure. Fortunately, her partner remained supportive, quietly taking on more household responsibilities. Looking back, she realises how much pressure she placed on herself. Her advice to other women? 'Get really clear on what's important in your life and what you truly want.'

The Early Years
Navigating the early stages of motherhood while balancing a career taught Farah invaluable lessons about managing household dynamics more effectively: 'Only two weeks after my daughter was born, I found myself thrown back into the whirlwind of daily life, which highlighted the need to simplify tasks and delegate responsibilities whenever possible. Recognising and leveraging each other's strengths and weaknesses within our partnership became essential to managing our home life.'

One adjustment was embracing online grocery shopping, which saved the time and effort by reducing frequent supermarket visits. 'Syncing calendars with my husband also became crucial, helping us stay informed about household commitments and schedules. Even with the support of a weekly cleaner, a privilege I'm acutely aware isn't accessible to everyone, the need for a shared approach to household tasks was clear. The division of chores between my husband and me is still a work in progress, but it's guided by a principle I hold dear: managing a home should never fall solely on one partner.'

Farah adds, 'Embracing shared responsibilities isn't just about fairness; it's about mutual respect and cooperation.' 'It lays the groundwork for a healthier, more balanced partnership, where both partners contribute to the home and each other's well-being.'

The School & Teenage Years

Sam is often asked how she managed as a mum with a demanding full-time career. 'I am always honest; it was a struggle, especially when my children started school. Primary school age was hard due to a lack of wraparound care, juggling school holiday care, and feeling awful when I forced my children into holiday clubs they didn't want to attend. I wasn't in a position to ask for parental leave as it wasn't financially viable. I was constantly on a war-footing, planning and re-planning.'

She adds: 'I observed how my male colleagues were often rewarded for taking time out for looking after their children, how they were applauded as dads. Whereas quite often I felt like I was living this secretive, dual life, flying slightly under the radar just so I could parent.'

Sam continues: 'The teenage years are hard in different ways, - navigating the pandemic, teenager mental health concerns, and guiding my daughter and now my son through GCSE's. It felt endless. At the same time my career was accelerating and then my mum became very ill. I felt pulled in every single direction with nothing left in the tank. I piled on weight. This was the moment I faced burnout. The day-to-day needs seemed endless. What helped me was being honest with myself about what I could or could not take on, but that was hard. I prided myself on being invincible. However, I had to make some tough decisions, inevitably leaving a loved corporate career to care for my terminally ill mum.'

Pauline's story is a common one. Now in her fifties with teenagers, she reflects on her childhood as the eldest of a large Irish family. After completing her master's, she entered the workforce and quickly became a marketing director. 'During my 20s, I wasn't even sure motherhood was my path. I was really focused on my career and being as successful as possible. Having spent much of my childhood looking after siblings, I wanted my independence.'

It wasn't until she met her partner and married that they decided to have children. Immediately afterward, she went back to work and requested part-time hours, which were denied without even a conversation. So, she left and found a new role that offered her some flexibility. 'There was always this pressure to go back to full-time hours, and eventually I decided to leave the company because I knew I wanted to be present and support my children. I sent myself out into the wilderness of freelancing and contract work.'

Pauline explains she was very lucky with her partner, who did a lot to support the family: 'We were a single unit without any family support around us, so we had to learn to communicate and work together. I recognise how fortunate I am compared to some other women in the same situation.'

Being a Single Parent

Anna, a CFO, found herself in the challenging position of being a single parent to two young children, aged 3 and 5, following a difficult divorce. 'My husband had an affair with a work colleague and left me just after my second child was born. He moved abroad with his then-girlfriend, leaving me to raise two young children on my own. My parents lived abroad,' she explained. 'At the time, I was a financial controller for a global pharmaceutical company. It was incredibly hard, dealing with the legal aspects of the divorce, selling our house, working and parenting full-time. My workplace was, and still is, amazing. My manager stepped in and said, "Go do what you need to do," allowing me to take time off whenever I needed it.'

Anna shared that she focused on building strong friendships during this time, creating a network that became essential for support. 'They weren't just shoulders to cry on, they became a community who could help. There were a few of us in the same boat, and we rallied around each other. One time, all our children came down with chickenpox, so we took turns taking days off to look after them.'

She recalled: 'However, each day was like a logistical puzzle, and sometimes, no matter how hard I tried, the pieces just wouldn't fit together.'

When asked about the impact on her career, she admits, 'My manager was brilliant, but the impact on my career was undeniable during those early years. I had to make a choice between my children and my career. Ultimately, my career took a back seat. I was part of a top talent programme that involved a lot of networking events and leadership development opportunities, but I had to pull out for three years.'

Anna continued: 'There were so many moments of guilt, for not fully pulling my weight at work and guilt for not being entirely present for my children. As soon as I could afford it, I hired an au pair, which allowed me to start refocusing on my career. Later, I found an amazing woman who became my fairy godmother, a housekeeper. Being able to rely on someone for help lifted a huge weight from my shoulders. I realise how privileged I am to afford this, and we sacrifice holidays abroad for it, but my housekeeper helps me stay sane and remain in the workforce.'

When asked if she considers this cost as a burden, effectively paying to work, Anna shares: 'It has crossed my mind, particularly when they were younger with the cost of childcare, I often felt like I was paying for the privilege of working as I was barely breaking even each month.'

She reflected on the emotional toll of being a single parent with no outside support. 'It is emotionally exhausting to be both parents with zero support. Asking for help was hard for me. I felt this expectation that I should just be able to do it all - magically. But asking for help and having my friends as a community around me was key.'

When asked how she manages everything, she adds: 'I've had to become a ruthless planner and organiser of menus, school, holidays, and life. I've also had to encourage my girls to be independent and organised as well. We work well as a team. I've learned to be very resilient. It's also made me exceptionally capable at work, nothing fazes me.

Anna acknowledges the gifts and wisdom these multiple roles have given her: 'Being a single parent is like being a CEO and I bring that into my work, every day. Our skills should not be underestimated.'

Parenting a Child with Additional Needs

Kathryn's journey as a mother to a child with additional needs has been defined by a determined pursuit of understanding, support, and advocacy for her autistic daughter.

Kathryn, a UK based compliance director in learning and development, recalls: 'From the moment she was born, my second daughter had health issues, including frightening episodes of sleep apnea where she would just stop breathing.'

Trusting her instincts, Kathryn embarked on a path toward diagnosis, a journey that required immense patience and perseverance. She adds: 'I learned early on that I had to be my child's biggest advocate. It was exhausting to fight with the school and ineffective council services just so my daughter could receive an Education and Healthcare Plan (EHCP) and the support she needs. My daily routines are anything but simple; even getting my child into school can be a battle, and that's all before I start my workday.'

The ongoing emotional and logistical balancing act has taken a toll on Kathryn's well-being, often leaving her feeling isolated and unsupported. She reflects on her previous job, where she worked for 20 years and had a particularly understanding manager with similar experiences. 'I would often turn up to work in tears or need to leave halfway through the day to pick up my daughter when she was struggling. There was a sisterhood there, and we had each other's backs. I wouldn't have gotten through those early days without that kind of support.'

However, Kathryn's experience changed when she moved to another company. 'I was told by one of the directors not to share my struggles about my daughter, in case it was used against me.'

The differing experiences highlight how essential a supportive work environment is for parents of children with additional needs.

Kathryn reflects on her upbringing, noting: 'I grew up in a time when my mum worked part-time, and my parents instilled in me the need to achieve not just in my career but also in keeping an immaculate home (so anyone could drop by at any time), and raising well-behaved children. When you don't have it all in some way, you can feel like a failure.'

What's evident from these stories is that there is not enough celebration and recognition for working mothers and the skills they develop and can bring to the workplace.

Motherhood is a masterclass in leadership, logistics, delegation and crisis management - yet these transferrable skills are undervalued and often invisible when it comes to our careers. Women who navigate the relentless demands of caregiving develop unmatched emotional intelligence, conflict resolution, time management, and decision making under pressure.

As the default CEOs of home and family, women negotiate, strategise and execute daily. We anticipate needs before they arise, manage competing priorities with precision and make high-stake decisions. This experience gives us an unparalleled ability to multi-task, problem solve and lead with empathy. We are as equally adept at dealing with toddler meltdowns as we are navigating the emotional turmoil and mental health needs of our teenagers or coaching our partners through life challenges. We can influence without authority and work across matrixed organisations - such as schools, healthcare and more.

These skills are the hallmark of exceptional 21st Century leadership. There is no one better suited to lead in a volatile, uncertain complex and ambiguous world. Yet instead of recognising this, corporate structures undervalue our contribution and penalise women for career breaks or flexible schedules. As Sam states: **'Women don't fall behind when they become mothers - we level up.'**

If we are to shatter the myth of 'doing it all, and being it all,' we must rewrite the rules and recognise that every woman's journey is unique and valuable. This is not about women working harder or men simply 'helping' at home - it's about creating meaningful structural change in our homes and workplaces, so that both women and men can achieve the balance they desire in their lives.

These are naturally complex and emotive subjects with a great deal of nuance. Firstly, invisible labour must be acknowledged; it requires men to step up and take responsibility, to be proactive rather than passive when comes to childcare and domestic labour. Secondly, it requires women to let men step up and without judgement. Reciprocal understanding and empathy can create space for much needed conversations, leading to shared dominions of support rather than separate spheres of work.

Furthermore, it requires workplaces to acknowledge the skills women bring to the table instead of penalising the time they take out to have children.

Recently on LinkedIn, D&I experts shared that the workplace is not the place for these conversations. **We disagree.** These conversations need to happen in schools, in the home and in the workplace. What's required is that we build the emotional agility to hold space for these conversations in a non-judgemental way and manage the emotions that inevitably arise without apportioning blame.

We simply cannot keep asking women to fix themselves - we are not broken. True change demands collective action, as the burden of change should not rest solely on women.

It is time for all of us to step up.

A Note for Male Allies

Parenthood is a huge shift for both men and women - but for women it can be significant - impacting career, earning potential and as well as mental and financial health. Run male ally circles to discuss these issues. Talk to your partner about the stories in this chapter, what has her experience been like? What else can you do to take over the cognitive load? Are you impacted by stigma related to taking parental leave? If you are a leader, what policies can you implement to support working parents and the women in your organisation?

Pause and Reflect

In what ways has the pursuit of 'having it all, doing it all and being it all' influenced your feelings about success and balance, as a parent? How might letting go of this myth change your perspective?

Reflect on the caregiving roles in your household or community. What shifts, big or small, could promote a more equitable division of responsibilities? Do you find yourself taking over?

How can you advocate for or contribute to systemic changes such as workplace policies or community initiatives, that better support working parents and caregivers?

'I am not a difficult woman at all.
I am simply a strong woman and know my worth'.
– Angelina Jolie

Chapter Seven
Transitioning

While not every woman will become a mother, nearly every biological female will experience the menopause. For some, it will happen naturally, even if prematurely; for others like Farah and Sam, it will happen surgically.

In *Women Who Run with the Wolves*, Dr Clarissa Pinkola Estés interprets the menopause as a significant transition that offers profound opportunities for personal growth and deeper self-awareness. Estés encourages women to view the menopause as not a loss but a vital period for reclamation, fostering creativity and renewed sense of purpose.

We believe the menopause is a transformative stage that moves beyond the physical, the energy we expel in menstruation ceases and we turn that energy inwards, signalling a deeper shift in identity, purpose and societal roles as we move into our *eldership*.

For the women who enter the menopause naturally, *The Climacteric*, the phase leading up to the menopause can intersect with significant life events: children leaving home, career shifts, caring for elderly relatives.

Whereas our grandmothers and mothers may have had children earlier and did not work, Gen X/Millennial women are often juggling with the trifecta of motherhood (tweens and teens), caring for elderly relatives and the peri/menopause just as they are heading into senior positions and career peaks. At best, it's a troublesome few years; at its worst, it's completely debilitating. For those of us who experience it surgically, it can bring a sudden onslaught of physical and emotional challenges at any age; there is no slow wind down but more of a sudden shock to the system.

Very often, by the time a woman has reached the menopause she is exhausted with the cumulative stress of career, caregiving, emotional labour. She may now be dealing with gendered ageism and financial insecurity. Some of our survey respondents mentioned feeling 'invisible', others shared how they felt they just had to power through, where any sign of struggle was a sign of weakness.

Sam has delivered hundreds of menopause women's circles over the past five years and now regards this phase of life differently to the negative, medicalised narrative that often surrounds it.

She shares: 'I've witnessed firsthand how transformative this part of our life journey can be. Women are not losing; they gain an inner wisdom, deepen their resilience and for some it can also bring clarity. However, we need to treat this phase with the respect and reverence it deserves.'

This time of our lives can be a liberation giving us an opportunity to reconnect with ourselves after years of caregiving and career building. A time to reclaim ourselves. Enabling the transition is key, celebrating it, owning it and understanding it, above all being kind to ourselves through it.

However, society needs to stop pushing women into shame and isolation; workplaces need to support it; and we need to give women knowledge early about their entire menstrual cycle and how to manage it.'

This phase can last about ten years and, according to the Faculty of Occupational Medicine, around one third of the entire UK population (13 million women) are currently peri or menopausal. It's estimated there will be 1.1 billion post-menopausal women in the world by 2025. In fact, menopausal women are the fastest growing demographic in the UK workforce,[lxxxii] with almost 8 out of 10 menopausal women in work.

Over the past 5 years, as more Gen X women move into this phase of their lives, several high-profile female celebrities have begun to share their menopause journey. Yet, it still feels like it's shrouded in secrecy and shame, much like menstruation.

As we researched this book, we found the menopause was treated differently around the world.

For example, in Japan, it's associated with years of renewal and regeneration. Women are celebrated through the tradition of 'Kanreki' and often receive gifts and participate in special ceremonies to commemorate this milestone.

The women of the Masai tribe of Kenya and Tanzania are celebrated through a ceremony called 'Emorata'. During this ceremony, women dress in traditional attire and gather to dance, sing, and share stories. The Emorata ceremony not only celebrates the woman's transition to a new stage of life but also serves to pass on cultural knowledge and wisdom to younger generations.

In some indigenous cultures, the menopause is seen as a powerful spiritual transformation and is often referred to as the 'wise woman' phase. Native American women are honored for their wisdom and are considered leaders and teachers within their communities.

It is a shame this same celebration isn't afforded to women in the western world. According to research published by the Chartered Institute of Personnel and Development (CIPD)[lxxxiii] in 2019, women faced significant challenges dealing with the menopause in the workplace. The study revealed that many women feel it negatively impacts their careers, resulting in reduced working hours, job loss, and increased instances of gendered ageism. This is despite organisations doing more to support women and menopause.

Data[lxxxiv] shows that menopausal women are at increased risk of suicide. In the US, the highest rates of female suicide are among those aged 45 – 64; the UK reports 45-49 years of age and Australia 45 – 49 years of age. Furthermore 42% of women consider quitting work because of their symptoms, 29% of women state their self-confidence was impacted at work or their menopause made them look incapable. 1 in 10 women are forced to leave their job because of their symptoms.

In our survey, 35% of our respondents reported to be in the menopause, 64% shared that they experienced negative impact to their careers and family life because of it and 24% of women shared that they had experienced significant impact to their career and family life. How and why are we allowing this to happen?

Sam was thrown into surgical menopause at the age of 27. Immediately put on HRT, she spent the next 20 years managing medication, mainly dealing with the side effects of Hot Flushes (called Hot Flashes in the US). In 2019, after a short HRT break, she noticed her menopause symptoms were far worse: brain fog, forgetfulness, anxiety - symptoms she hadn't experienced previously.

She shared: 'Admittedly life was more stressful, caring for teenagers, caring for elderly parents and a full-time leadership role, but I felt 1000 times worse. I thought I had early onset dementia. I went to my doctor where we discovered that chronic stress was making my menopause symptoms worse.'

At the same time, Sam was diagnosed with ADHD, she says: 'This was, to date, one of the hardest periods of my life. I've navigated cancer, infertility, job changes and moving country. The menopause and its emotional toll took this to a whole new level. I lost so much confidence. I was utterly exhausted, and I felt desperately alone. I kept wondering if my family would be better off without me.'

There are hundreds of stories like this.

Sam recalls one of the participants in a women's circle she ran talking about how she was mandated to come into the office, despite experiencing awful menopausal flooding that regularly saturated her clothes.

'This poor woman had to travel via public transport and felt unsafe to leave her home. Her manager, who happened to be the HR director, demanded she show up to the office, despite being fully aware of what this woman was going through. She told me she had to choose between going to work or quitting, and she was distraught because she loved her job and was terrified about what the financial implications might mean, including the real risk of losing her home. It seems we lack humanity when it comes to supporting women at times like these.'

Recently, in the UK, the Equality and Human Rights Commission [lxxxv] issued guidance to clarify the legal obligations to workers going through the menopause. Failure to make reasonable adjustments amounts to disability discrimination. Yet, just like with other reasonable adjustments, many women feel unsafe asking for them. We need more education and empathy in our relationships and workplaces to support women through this phase of their lives. This includes mandating all UK Health Insurers offer menopause services as a routine part of their package, so women do not incur additional costs.

Access to medical care is painful and despite more education and some menopause support being placed at GP practices in the UK, it's still a postcode lottery approach to healthcare, and it's still a one-size-fits-all.

The truth is women require regular blood tests to monitor their hormone levels, but it's not part of the protocol unless you can afford it. Our endocrine system is like a Formula 1 car, with hormones so finely tuned to meet our individual needs - it is not a one size fits all - some women need testosterone and HRT whilst others sail through the menopause without a problem. Those who can afford to opt to go privately to see specialist menopause doctors. But all this still amounts to a cost to women, another gender penalty we must pay and labour through.

Women should not have to choose between the menopause or career. With the right support, medication, a caring and aware partner, and understanding workplace, women can transition successfully through the menopause. Forcing women to leave their positions due to a lack of support is another form of systemic oppression and discrimination.

Through our research, we heard countless stories of women who had experienced discrimination because of their menopausal symptoms, such as women being placed on performance improvement plans and clumsily exited from the workplace.

In 2021, *The Guardian*[lxxxvi] shared Mara's story, a woman thrust into surgical menopause after a hysterectomy for endometriosis. She was overwhelmed by debilitating brain fog, anxiety, and depression. 'I was drowning,' she said. 'I couldn't see or think.'

Despite being prescribed antidepressants and oestrogen gel, nothing helped. She struggled to function at work, unable to retain information or think clearly. When she informed her supervisors of her depression, they placed her on a performance warning. Unaware menopause was the root cause, she felt ashamed and incapable. Even after a specialist confirmed her symptoms were menopause-related, her employer continued to penalise her.

Weekly meetings reinforced her perceived failures, pushing her to the brink. One summer afternoon, after a day out with her family, she drove to a motorway bridge, ignoring frantic calls from her husband. 'It wasn't that I wanted to die,' she later shared. 'I needed to die. Work wasn't ever going to stop doing what they were doing to me.'

As MP Caroline Nokes shared in an online article, 'Women over 50 are the fastest growing group in the workforce. These are highly skilled, experienced role models at the peak of their careers. The workforce is haemorrhaging these talented women, forcing them to reduce their hours or leave work entirely.'

One of our interviewees shared this: 'I thought as a female, the hardest time of my life, being a working mum, was possibly over, it seems not.'[lxxxvii]

Another common problem is the dismissal of menopausal symptoms by the medical profession. A form of 'gaslighting' as some of our survey respondents called it. Menopausal symptoms are often misdiagnosed as psychiatric issues, with many women forced onto inappropriate treatments, such as antidepressants.

Even worse, studies into menopause treatment, suggest that a third of women wait up to 3 years before their symptoms are correctly diagnosed. It's astonishing that over half the population are being treated in this manner, and yet a simple hormone test could easily accelerate the outcome and help women lead better lives as they transition.

This transitional phase forces many women inward to examine their lives. According to research by the Family Law

Menopause Project [lxxxviii] and Newson Health, [lxxxix] the menopause period is cited as a reason for the breakdown of marriages.

Sam's view: 'I struggle with us pinning the blame solely on a woman's hormonal activity. Yes, chaotic hormone levels put us in a temporary whirlwind. But what I often find is that women are at their most reflective at this age and for many the pressure cooker lid explodes. Out pours years of oppression, discrimination, the burden of being the primary carer, and the one who takes on the brunt of the emotional labour. Women use this time to reassess whether having it all was ever realistic or even desirable. Women have had enough.'

Sam continues: 'The lack of self-care, loneliness, grief with the loss of parents, children leaving home - spark the sudden realisation that women are into the next phase of their lives. Menopausal rage explodes like hot lava, and it can be destructive and cleansing at the same time.'

She adds: 'I coach a lot of women and after years of putting themselves on the back burner, some are completely lost and suicidal, some start reclaiming themselves. In tandem, many of them find themselves abandoned by their employers as gendered ageism rears its head. There is a lot of emotion and confusion as women yet again navigate a harsh landscape - often alone.'

Sam concludes: 'It's not the menopause that's the cause; it is western societies lack of care for women throughout their lives. We reach a boiling point, and most women feel enough is enough, and they seek to change what is not working. In my corporate roles, a lot of male colleagues came and asked for help. They were struggling to deal with this new phase in their personal lives, worried for their partners, concerned about their relationships, and unsure how to navigate it.'

We need to educate our menfolk about the menopause, not just the medical side of it, but the emotional layers that women are peeling off as they journey through it. I always say communication, empathy, and self-education are key. Men need to do their work through this too. This can be an incredible opportunity for men and women to winter together.'

There is light at the end of the tunnel. A research study[xc] suggests women aged 50-70 years of age are much happier, post-menopause. The physical and mental challenges associated with the that peri and menopausal period dissipate, and women begin to feel free and find renewed energy and optimism. As author and gynecologist, Dr Mary Claire Haver shared in a podcast, 'Women find this power to put themselves first for the first time in their adult lives; their give-a-shit factor goes away. They don't care anymore.'

However, the empowerment post-menopausal women feel can be a double-edged sword. Dr Lucy Ryan, author of *Revolting Women*, discovered mid-life women are quitting the workforce for three reasons: 1) the maintenance of power; 2) the collision of mid-life changes, and 3) a revolution against gendered ageism.

The impact of this cannot be underestimated - leaving the workforce impacts our financial wealth and puts us at greater risk of losing our homes and financial stability. It also impacts the future of society. If there is no diversity at the top of organisations, people making decisions for business, technology strategy, culture, and society remain largely white and male, and we forgo role models for the upcoming generations.

Farah concludes, 'These women are in the prime of their lives, they are the trailblazers and role models for younger women in the workplace. What are we telling our daughters and our sons if we won't support their mothers?'

Transitioning through Empty Nests
Suzanna's mom always told her that parenting was one giant 'letting go'. As Suzanna's own teenagers move into the phase of 'leaving home', she feels this internal conflict: 'On the one hand, I am excited for them as they step into this phase of their lives, grateful they've made it, that they are decent humans. I give myself a pat on the back for parenting them this far, especially as a single mom. And there is a part of me that is looking forward to reclaiming parts of my life and having time for me.'

'On the other hand, boy, the anticipatory grief has been hard. I cry when I walk past their bedrooms, and they aren't there.

This is the first year, both my boys are at college.' Suzanna adds: 'For the first three months, I was in full grief mode. I felt like I had lost my limbs and didn't want to be that mom who was calling or facetiming all the time. No one had prepared me for this. I am lucky, I have a bunch of great friends and one of them could see I was struggling. She wrapped her arms around me, metaphorically, and kept me occupied. I think the hardest part was more than not being physically around; it was the loss of structure, meaning, and purpose. As parents, especially mothers, we give so much of ourselves and to our kids. I found volunteering and community work helped.'

Jackie's story, similar in some ways, illustrates how this transition can impact relationships. 'I have one child, a daughter. She left home to go to Uni in Edinburgh and then went to travel the world. I haven't seen her physically in a year. This past year was the hardest, but I threw myself into work, grateful I had a very full-on senior role as an Alliances Director in a tech company. I found a new freedom, being able to travel more and take on more evening & networking responsibilities not feeling guilty that I was away as much.'

Jackie continued: 'However, the space that was now in my life shone a light on how broken my marriage was. Both my partner and I were just kind of lodgers in the same home and lodgers in our marriage. We were together out of convenience. It took one weekend for us to feel like strangers in our own home, a really awkward weekend, where we didn't know what to say to each other. My partner is typically avoidant, and I had to engineer a heart-to-heart so we could address what was happening.'

There was a lot of soul searching. I questioned if I still wanted to be in this relationship or throw away twenty plus years of living with someone. We ended up in couples therapy, which was the best decision we made. Nine months later, we are happier than ever. We're learning to be together again as well as respecting each other's individuality, and it's fun. We have more money to spend on ourselves as well.'

The feelings of grief, loss of purpose, emptiness and questioning identity are commonplace in this transition phase, especially for mother's whose primary role has been caregiving. In researching and talking to women, one of the ways to reframe this process is to see it as an invitation to nurture oneself, finding new hobbies or career paths.

In her book, *Second Spring: A Woman's guide to a New Season*, Kate Codrington, discusses the seasons of perimenopause and the menopause, where perimenopause is autumn and menopause is winter. Whilst there is a surrender to healing, transitioning, and going inwards, we know that during winter new green shoots are emerging under the surface, and this pushes us toward our second spring. A menopausal adolescence - a rebirthing.

Psychologist Carl Jung's theory of individuation suggests middle age is a time when people can move toward self-actualisation, where women can embrace the empty nest phase as an opportunity for deeper self-reflection. When combined with active strategies such as renewing friendships, deepening spousal connections, finding new activities and purpose, this phase can transition from empty to fulfilling.

Tips to help you Transition:
- **Reframe this time** and shift your mindset from loss to growth.
- **Establish new daily rituals** focused on self-care and wellbeing.
- **This can be a great time to learn** something new or take up an old hobby.
- **If you are in a relationship,** schedule meaningful time together.
- **Make time** for friends and family.
- **Get a dog -** as one of our interviewees shared; this saved her when both her children left home.
- **Find your silver lining** when you find it hard to navigate; gratitude work can help reset

Transitioning through Loneliness
Lorna sat in circle with us at a woman's retreat in Devon with tears flowing down her face. A MedTech start up Chief Marketing Officer, a mum and stepmum to four children (aged 14-20), who lived with her and her partner full-time, Lorna spent a lot of her time travelling between Europe and the Silicon Valley.

Lorna was lonely. Her life was a treadmill of motherhood, work, and marriage, underpinned by frequent travel. She loved her career and being a mum, but there was no spare time for friendships. She struggled to maintain her existing ones and felt guilty when she was out of the country and unable to attend friends' birthdays and other events. She lived in a wealthy area of southeast UK, and many of her son's childhood friends were stay-at-home mums, and she felt she had nothing in common with them.

As Lorna sat in circle, she shared: 'I just want that special person or people I can connect with, a community, someone I can share what's going on in my life and have meaningful conversations with. Someone who cares enough to ask me how my day is and lets me moan about my work, kids, or husband.

'I want someone I can chat to or go see romcoms with when I am in town. I am worried what will happen when I start to slow down. I worry I'll have zero friends and struggle to find new ones. I feel awful moaning about it, as I realise how lucky I am to have my family, and a truly brilliant career, but there is something extra special about real-life friendships that I miss.'

Loneliness is a growing challenge that affects people of all ages, particularly during life transitions. Despite being more digitally connected, we are increasingly disconnected, attached to our phones and starved for real affection. The loneliness epidemic has severe health consequences, with research showing that loneliness can mislead hormonal signals, worsening health conditions like menopause and increasing the risk of illness. Emotional isolation is as lethal as smoking, and studies suggest cancer can metastasize faster in lonely people.

A 2023[xci] study found 53% of women in the workplace experience loneliness, with rates increasing as they climb the corporate ladder. Ann Shoket, CEO of TheLi.st, observed that many women feel lonely because of their jobs, with nearly 60% reporting increased isolation as their careers progress.

Women experience loneliness more than men, although unmarried men tend to feel lonelier than unmarried women. According to Richard V. Reeves, men often rely on women emotionally due to patriarchal structures, and as women gain economic independence, men struggle emotionally. This risks further burdening women with men's emotional care at the expense of their own well-being.[xcii]

Women will often neglect to invest in friendships along with self-care as there are not enough hours in the day to do it all and be it all. Sam found a path by joining women's circles online during the pandemic.

She says, 'I found an organisation called *Global Sisterhood* and they held women's circles online. I loved being part of a small group. Initially, I was just grateful to have a space to be heard and to feel I could be authentically me; then it became about learning from indigenous female elders from across the world, which was magical and then finding deep friendships with other women. I now make it a priority to attend women's retreats as well as holding women's circles.'

Humans need social connection. We have, according to psychologist, Mark Leary, a 'need to belong'. There is an imperative to ensure women find support and belonging with one another to stave off the impact of loneliness. But as we have seen throughout this book, prioritising relationships, when women are having to do it all and be it all is almost impossible.

Tips to help you transition into you:
- **Define what you need.** Get clear on what you want/need from your network. Some people love solitude but acknowledge when this turns into loneliness. love our alone time. Reflect when you feel most isolated.
- **Find online communities.** Online communities can be sources of great support. Just ensure to make time for in-person connection as well.
- **Find your passion.** Is there something you dreamed of doing but never had the time to fit it in? Now is that time. Make it a reality, you'll be surprised who you meet.
- **Volunteering** is a great way to meet new people, particularly if you can support other lonely people in your community.
- Work out how to **schedule friendship** into your life and contract with your friends on frequency and

supporting one another through the hard times. Communication is key in these spaces.
- If you are feeling really isolated with low mood, **seek professional help, don't struggle alone.**

Re-finding yourself, your worth and your identity.
After navigating a challenging divorce and being made redundant last year, Louise felt completely lost. 'I wasn't sure who I was anymore. I was 54 years old, jobless, partnerless. I don't have any children, I had no anchor, and I had a breakdown. My work was everything, possibly too much, and my identity was tied to my role and status.'

She continues: 'I felt a lot of shame at being made redundant, and there was a grieving process. I had been at the company for nearly 30 years and the people there were my family; some of the younger ones were like my own children. When you go through a redundancy process, it's emotionally hard. I felt cast out, and a lot of my "friendships" dried up overnight. I was lucky because I had my blood relatives, siblings, their children, and some close friendships to move myself through it. But I had to do a lot of work to let go of my ego and reconnect with me, re-find my new purpose and what I stood for.'

When asked how she moved herself through this period, she shared: 'I spent a lot of time focusing on my strengths and skills, reading self-help books, and listening to a lot of podcasts. I sought therapy and a coach, I reviewed my values to focus on what I cared about, not the values I had assumed. I created a vision board with a list of the top 40 things I wanted to achieve before I was 80. This gave me a strong sense of autonomy and put some fire back in my soul.

'The hard part was trying to find a new role. I encountered a lot of discrimination due to my age and possibly my gender. I wasn't looking for high flying corporate roles anymore and found employers wouldn't bother giving me a second interview. Some of them said I was too overqualified. That rejection was hard.'

A lot of the women we surveyed and spoke to shared they had lost sight of their sense of self as they juggled multiple roles and this impacted their perspective of having it all, for some it redefined what success looked like, for others, they grew more anxious as if time was running out to achieve it all.

When life events happen, gaps appear leaving a self-identity struggle. Psychologist Erik Erikson's stages of psychosocial development suggest that later life is characterised by the need for 'ego integrity'. This stage of life offers a wonderful opportunity to rediscover your soul, your worth, and your identity outside of traditional societal roles.

Martha Beck's *Finding your own North Star* emphasises how reconnecting with your true self is essential for emotional health and fulfilment. Having purpose is important as we traverse into eldership, there is a lot of research that shows having a sense of purpose can help us to stay healthier for longer and lowers the risk of chronic conditions and premature mortality.[xciii]

Farah and Sam both believe that this liminal space is incredibly potent for women. They can regain a sense of self, strength, identity, marking out a new self-expression. As Farah points out, 'The menopause is often talked about in terms of loss, but we need to learn to rewrite this narrative for ourselves. We're living longer, so we may spend up to 38 years or more post-menopausal. We shouldn't be afraid of setting ourselves up for success, both emotionally, romantically and financially.'

Many women can find this time brings up lots of emotional memories, especially if they haven't dealt with past events/trauma properly or with the passing of loved ones. Our own fears around mortality can arise. Remember, it's not selfish to focus attention on oneself for once.

Tips to help you transition:

- **Reassess** what is important to you. Do values work and redefine what you need or want from this next phase of your life.
- **Identify** YOUR passions.
- Set realistic short-term **goals** that align with your rediscovered identity.
- If you are reading this as a mid-30s woman, **plan** for this future time. Sam calls it the 3rd phase. Feel empowered to own and reclaim it.
- **Look at your lifestyle**. This is a great time to embed healthy habits.
- **Define your purpose**. If we have given so much to caregiving or working, we can lose purpose. Take

some steps to re-define this. This is a time to centre yourself.

Transitioning Careers: Letting go and managing ageism
'I am seeking peace and freedom… perhaps even a new challenge? If I am honest, I've had enough of the politics and game playing. I've begun to find that each quarter and year-end blur into one another.' Aged 60, Christine has spent all her life working in corporate roles, starting out in marketing, then moving into sales.

For the past ten years, she has been Vice President of Sales for a large European organisation. 'I'm not ready to retire. I feel I have so much experience to share and lots to give. But the shine of infinite growth and battling the same challenges and ego's each quarter has lost its edge. Plus, there are not a lot of women like me at these levels. I am still ambitious, and I need to work for financial stability. However, I also want to spend some time on things that fulfil me.'

When asked what's stopping her, she shared: 'I don't feel I have a lot of choice. Friends of mine who are impacted by redundancy are struggling to find employment. One of my acquaintances worked as a HR director and has had to take a role at Waitrose (a UK supermarket) because she can't find a job that offers her part-time work at a senior level. We've dealt with this discrimination all our lives and it's exhausting.'

Christine continues: 'I would LOVE to work less hours. I really want to go back and study for a master's in fine art and do some more travelling. I've worked full-time since I left school, even when I had my daughter. My role requires lots of travel to see customers and teams across Europe and that often eats into my weekends.' She adds: 'When I proposed a sabbatical two years ago, it was pushed out due to an acquisition and the need for all hands-on deck. I can't afford to just 'give up' work, and I don't want to do that. I still feel I have lots of value to add. But I'd like to do it in a more balanced way.'

Christine has asked her leader if a part-time role is possible, and the reception has been frosty. 'There is a very old school way of thinking that leaders must be full-time. Interestingly, I know lots of male leaders who spend a lot of time on golf courses and at their second homes, barely working full-time. I know I am capable of running a business with the team I have hired and doing it 3 days a week. I really don't want to restart somewhere else at this level.' She ends: 'We risk losing some great, experienced women in the workplace; you can't just replace that kind of experience. Organisations lose so much inherent knowledge by not offering more flexible working options and viewing that in a positive light.'

Transitioning into new careers or roles is hard at any age, but it can feel much harder with age. Workplace ageism is a persistent barrier. Studies show ageism impacts women disproportionately often manifesting as negative stereotypes about older employees' abilities. In the UK, 67% of women over 50 are in the workforce, an increase of 20% since 2000.

As we write this chapter, data from a recent survey to mark the 70th Anniversary of the Women of the Year Lunch and Awards indicates most women still experience the same workplace challenges we did in the 90's. The survey also highlighted a growing concern around ageism, with 1 in 3 of the highflyer women aged 51+ reporting they had directly experienced age-related discrimination.

In truth, women experience gendered ageism throughout our working lives. We're either too young, going to get pregnant, destined to transition into menopause, or we're too old when viewed through the lens of ageing skin, greying hair, post-reproductive status and alleged brain fog.

Sam shares her perspectives: 'We need to push organisations harder against ageism in their workforce. I know women are not the only one's experiencing the issue. Gen X employees are beginning to experience a huge shock as they are made redundant or seek new roles elsewhere. This demographic is often very loyal with minimal distractions and have a heap of experience.

Sam recommends planning for this 'Second Spring'. 'Just as we are taught to plan as we onramp into our careers, I believe we need to plan to offramp too. We're told to plan for retirement, but we're not empowered or educated to plan for this specific period of our lives–pre-retirement.'

Given existing challenges around ageism, the lack of meaningful change in the 9 to 5, it's likely women reading this book will experience redundancy, forced out of their careers, or quit around this age. The advice is to take back our power and plan for this part of our lives. It's vital we also resist our own internalised ageism by reclaiming personal narratives. We can store so much of our identity based on our careers and roles and find that hard to let go. Building self-confidence and maintaining a strong sense of worth helps women challenge common stereotypes.

Tips to help you Transition:

- **Stay professionally relevant** through ongoing education and skills training; keep up with the latest technology.
- **Explore flexible work arrangements.** Find out if that's possible for elder workers and, if not, see if you can champion it.
- **Review a portfolio career on your terms:** This may give you the challenge, excitement, and financial security you need in this phase. Advisory, Non-Executive Director, Consultancy and Freelance options are all potential ways to support this phase.
- If you are considering retirement, **talk to your employer about a phased retirement plan**, whereby you get to continue to add value, and they retain institutional knowledge whilst preparing for exit.
- **Put your needs first**. Create your second spring plan.
- Don't neglect financial planning.

Let's reclaim the menopause as not simply an ending but a powerful beginning an opportunity to transition on our terms. It marks a time of profound personal growth, introspection, and, for many women, a chance to refactor their lives. In a society that has long been silent on the realities of the menopause, it is critical we now challenge the cultural narrative that shrouds this transition in shame and secrecy.

It's vital we bring men into the menopause conversation. This period of a woman's life can affect relationships and families. It is essential men educate themselves. The physical and emotional changes brought on by menopause can profoundly impact romantic relationships, often leading to misunderstandings, distance and conflict.

Many men feel unprepared to support their partners, unsure of how to respond to mood shifts, changes in intimacy and fatigue. Without awareness these challenges can strain the strongest partnerships. Research shows that a lack of communication contributes to increased divorce rates during this time. In our last chapter we highlighted the impact of how masculinity can downplay emotional connection and vulnerability, this is a time when men need to lean in and take time to learn about the symptoms and acknowledge the emotional toll we experience and journey it together in our homes and work.

The stories of the women in this chapter highlight the struggles and opportunities within this journey. As workplaces begin to slowly recognise the needs of menopausal women, much more must be done to support this rapidly growing demographic. Empowering women to transition through this phase with confidence and dignity should not be an afterthought but a priority for all facets of society, government, business, healthcare, and beyond. It's time to reclaim our narrative, our bodies, and our lives.

By reframing the menopause as a period of wisdom, freedom, and self-reclamation, we open the door to greater understanding and support for women in all walks of life, we also create the opportunity for women to achieve what they want.

The journey through the menopause is not just one of biological change but a time of liberation, an opportunity to regain power, purpose, and joy.

A Note to Male Allies

Any man reading this book will have a female relative, loved one or colleague experience the menopause. There is a real opportunity to 'do the work' and learn about the menopause and what women will go through and how best to support them. If you are a leader: Ensure there are adequate menopause policies in place and work to destigmatise how the menopause is perceived, ensure reasonable accommodations are supported. Work hard to eradicate gendered ageism. Empathy is a crucial part of this journey. This is a great time to engage allies in conversation about how it is affecting them.

Partnering through the Transition

It is thanks to Gen X women that the menopause is being discussed more openly. However, for many men, the menopause is a still a mystery shrouded in silence. If you are in a relationship, your partner may notice your emotions or that you are struggling with symptoms but not connect it to the menopause. Unlike pregnancy, the menopause is invisible and unpredictable. Furthermore, men were never taught about it at school and society does not normalise conversations about aging in women, or even menstruation in women. This means men simply do not know how to support us and may fear getting it wrong and leads to avoidance rather than engagement.

It is not your responsibility to educate, but you can invite your partner into the conversation, whilst setting expectations they take ownership for their own learning. Do not be afraid to ask for support. It is important to remember, none of us are mind-readers, yet.

Pause and Reflect

As you reflect on your life's journey, what parts of yourself have you set aside to meet societal, familial, or career expectations? How might you reconnect with those lost or overlooked aspects of your identity during this transformative phase?

During significant transitions, whether menopause, career shifts, or changes in family dynamics, what does a fulfilled and meaningful life look like for you now? What small steps can you take to align your daily actions with this vision?

What practices or communities could you embrace to foster resilience and create a supportive network during this phase? How can you prioritise your emotional and physical well-being while navigating the challenges you face?

'I view Menopause as a second adolescence. You finally have time to put yourself first and decide what you really want to do'.
-Jane Fonda

A New Dawn for Women in the 21st Century

Part Three

Chapter Eight
Breaking the Silence

#1 - Silence by History: The Historical Suppression of Women's Voices

What is it about women's voices that makes ideologies, workplaces, relationships and history fear them? Our voices have been systemically silenced, erased from history, excluded from power and dismissed in public and private spheres.

Every human came from a female body, yet nothing on earth is shamed or criticised as much.

Strong women in society evoke a complex mix of admiration, resistance, and misunderstanding. Often celebrated for their resilience, leadership, and ability to break barriers, they serve as role models in various fields, from politics and entrepreneurship to activism. However, deeply ingrained gender norms and stereotypes frequently mischaracterise assertiveness as aggression or independence as a threat to traditional expectations.

This 'double bind' forces strong women to navigate a fine line between being perceived as too soft or too tough, often subjecting them to heightened scrutiny. While we challenge patriarchal structures and inspire progress, we also face backlash, isolation, or tokenism, particularly in male-dominated fields. Intersectional factors like race and class further complicate our experiences, as biases intersect and amplify our challenges.

Despite these obstacles, strong women continue to embody courage and determination, redefining strength and pushing the boundaries of gendered expectations, even as they navigate the persistent pressures to conform to unattainable standards of 'having it all'.

Historian Mary Beard documents in her book *Women & Power* how deeply embedded this suppression of women's voices is in our western culture. In ancient Greece and Roman times, women were barred from education, public speech and leadership roles, their voices deemed unworthy of civic discourse that defined democracy. This suppression laid the groundwork for centuries of patriarchal control.

In Medieval Europe, women who formed healing communities, practiced midwifery, or shared herbal remedies were often labelled as witches. Accusations of witchcraft were strategically deployed to dispossess women of their land and property. This tactic was widespread amongst widows or those without male heirs, and especially widespread in 1692 during the Salem Witch Trials. Scholars like Silvia Federici argue witch hunts were a means to suppress resistance to the loss of common land and enforce new economic structures, removing our economic independence and social standing and relegating women to the domestic sphere only.[xciv]

In the US, during the 1830's, The Lowell Mill Girls, young factory women, formed one of the first labour unions and were labelled as unruly and disruptive as they attempted to self-advocate. They faced harsh suppression as they spoke out for equal rights.

The Irish Magdalen Laundries, operating between the 18th to 20th Centuries, are another harrowing example of how society and religion silenced and controlled women. Women who were unmarried mothers, victims of assault, deemed promiscuous or simply defied social norms were forcibly confined, often for life and their children stolen from them.

As women came together during the suffragette movement in the late 19th/early 20th Century, demanding the right to vote, they were categorised as unfeminine, hysterical or threatening to society. In fact, anti-suffragette propaganda often depicted suffragettes as neglectful mothers and wives to isolate women from the movement. Again, in the 19th Century, Cambridge university in the UK exercised authority over local women through the 'Spinning House' a private prison where unchaperoned women could be detained without trial.

In the 1960's and 70's, during second wave feminism, women advocating and marching for workplace rights, reproductive rights and equality faced unforgiving criticism. Women who joined these movements were labelled 'man-haters or radicals.' The tactics used aimed to delegitimise their cause and divide women. Women of colour who were advocating for intersectionality within the movement were often sidelined, highlighting the deliberate fragmentation of female solidarity.

Today the silencing of women continues in chillingly overt forms under regimes across the world.

This suppression of our voices is also mirrored in subtler yet equally dangerous ways in modern societies, where female survivors of domestic and sexual violence are met with disbelief, victim-blamed or where in modern workplaces women who speak out are silenced through legal mechanisms such as non-disclosure agreements (NDAs).

Yet, as Audre Lorde reminds us in her essay, *The Transformation of Silence into Language and Action*, silence is not merely a symptom of oppression, it is a tool of control that fractures women's psyches and perpetuates cycles of shame, fear and isolation, breaking the bonds of sisterhood and connection. For many women who speak up, breaking the silence is an act of resistance met with further marginalisation.

The 2017 #MeToo movement ushered in a global reckoning, shining a light on the epidemic of sexual violence, uniting women globally to speak out against harassment and assault. Yet it faced significant backlash, detractors labelled it as divisive, extreme and harmful to men, should they be falsely accused.

This narrative yet again attempting to discredit the collective power of women sharing their stories and reclaiming their voices.

While social media has empowered women to connect, it is also used as a tool to divide. When women speak up online, they are often threatened with rape, murder or cancelled. In today's AI, Deepfake world, our images are stolen and superimposed on the bodies of naked women and sent around the internet to humiliate or blackmail us. Women are pitted against one another labelled 'Karen's', mum-shamed, or held to ridiculous beauty standards.

Today, just as women's communities in corporate spaces have begun to have impact, an 'anti-diversity' backlash has sprung up with some proclaiming diversity and inclusion as unfair. This silencing of women, be it through ancient systems of exclusion, theocratic oppression, or societal and relational gaslighting, denies women their humanity, agency and the ability to rewrite their own stories and as Audre Lorde reminds us:

> 'there's always a little piece inside of you that wants to be spoken out, and if you keep ignoring it, it gets madder and madder and hotter and hotter and if you don't speak it out one day it will just up and punch you in the mouth.'

There are numerous psychological and physical impacts of this historical and current silencing. We're aware through research that trauma can be transmitted through generations. Thanks to studies of epigenetics, environmental factors, like trauma can affect gene expression without altering DNA, impacting cortisol regulation and how we regulate our stress response. Fear and hypervigilance can be transmitted to offspring, leading to increased anxiety and sensitivity to stress.

The witch hunts, for example, were not just acts of violence against women, they could be seen as acts of psychological warfare aimed at dismantling female solidarity and community knowledge, creating intergenerational consequences such as distrust, isolation, internalised misogyny, loss of knowledge, cultural conditioning, internalised silence, hypervigilance and cultural amnesia.

Conducting a short internet search, we can find hundreds of programmes aimed at helping women to 'find their voice, be heard, live authentically'. Sam observes the many women who come to her for coaching and sit in circle, 'being heard and having a voice are core needs and from a psychological, social and cultural perspective, the ability to express ourselves and have that expression acknowledged are fundamental to our well-being, personal identity and social connection.'

She adds: 'As the author Dr Edith Eger states the opposite of depression is expression. What comes out of our body doesn't make us ill, what stays in there does. I see women physically change when they are heard and find their voice.'

Breaking the silence plays a key role in shattering the myth of 'having it all, doing it all, and being it all.' It's not just a symbolic act but a radical reclamation of our power, or as Gloria Steinem suggests an 'outrageous act and everyday rebellion.'

No matter how we choose to use our voices in classrooms, writing, relationships, communities, politics or workspaces, we do so knowing that sharing stories helps us to dismantle what holds us back and set us free and allow us to re-write our history and our future. Breaking the silence is what we owe to ourselves, our mothers and future generations.

#2 – Silenced by the Law: The Hidden cost of NDAs & Discrimination

Our survey revealed a troubling pattern amongst the women who responded, 60% reported having to file a grievance at work. Further research revealed approximately 42% of US working women have faced job-related discrimination due to gender, with issues ranging from pay disparity to insufficient support from leadership.[xcv]

This trend is mirrored in the UK, research from the Trade Union Congress (TUC) reveals that nearly one in two women have experienced sexual harassment at work, yet a significant number remain silent, fearing retaliation or job loss. Similarly, across Europe, studies indicate a high incidence of gender discrimination, with the European Institute for Gender Equality noting persistent challenges in achieving workplace equality.

To maintain confidentiality, we will refer to one remarkable woman as Sofia. A captain for a leading global airline, Sofia navigates the complexities of balancing a demanding career with a young family. Sofia shares the challenges of being away from home due to her work, acknowledging it is tough to be apart from her daughter and husband. 'I know she occasionally gets sad when I'm not there,' she says of her daughter. 'Balancing my professional life with family time is crucial. Having adult time and my work is important for me, so I have to balance that with making the most of the days we have together when I'm at home.'

Her work schedule, consisting of random days, allows for unique opportunities to spend time with her daughter. Recently, she transitioned to short-haul flights, which enables her to be at home more and avoid the exhaustion of night flights.

Support systems play a vital role in Sofia's ability to manage both professional and personal responsibilities. After her daughter was born, she chose to work part-time. 'I also have a very supportive husband who luckily can be flexible with his time, and he does the childcare when I'm at work if our daughter isn't at nursery,' she shares. Additionally, her mother provides childcare support on days when her husband is unavailable.

Despite the support, Sofia has encountered discrimination in her career. The aviation industry, where only about 5% of pilots are women, still harbours strong stereotypes. 'This means a lot of people assume I'm not a pilot or can't believe I'm a pilot, even when in my uniform,' she recounts. She hopes more women will enter aviation and serve as role models for younger girls.

Discrimination also manifests in professional interactions and policies. 'We definitely get forgotten,' she states, highlighting the ongoing struggle for improved maternity pay and policies in aviation, which lag behind other professions. She has also experienced direct sexism from male colleagues. 'I have been ignored by male ground staff before who have not seen me as the captain and gone to the most senior male cabin crew to liaise with them instead.'

Further conversations with women revealed when they speak up, they frequently face professional retaliation, while perpetrators remain undisturbed and employed, particularly leaders. Many of the women we spoke to who experienced these issues felt no choice but to leave their employment, some indicated being 'managed out' through performance programmes or offered settlements to leave.

In these extreme cases, restrictive legal tools and processes such as Non-Disclosure Agreements (NDAs) continue to silence women, trapping them in a cycle of secrecy and disempowerment. NDAs, initially designed to protect trade secrets are frequently employed in workplace settlements, particularly in cases involving discrimination, harassment or bullying.

Whilst NDAs may offer short-term resolution and compensation, they often leave systemic injustices unchallenged, suppressing workplace misconduct and whistleblowing.

Just as we see perpetrators of gender-based violence and sexual assault often walk free, in society, so we see the similar issues play out in the workplace.

In fact, we believe NDAs reflect and perpetuate broad systemic issues, such as the ongoing under valuing of women's contributions in the workplace and the normalisation of power imbalances.

Having listened to these stories, we feel very strongly it's time to break the silence on these hidden legal mechanisms. Organisations and leaders have a major role to play in the success of women and their careers, not just through sponsorship, mentoring or allyship, but by creating real change.

Diversity programmes promised to deliver but were often a hastily crafted band-aid, a visual prop, with no real teeth to cut through bias and possibly no real desire for change. To deliver meaningful change requires driving accountability at all layers of an organisation and dealing swiftly with transgressions.

The #MeToo movement shone a light on NDA abuse. The campaign group, *Can't Buy My Silence*, was set up when co-founder Zelda Perkins became the first woman to break an NDA, signed decades earlier, with Harvey Weinstein. *Can't*

Buy My Silence believe NDAs have become the default solution for organisations, corporations and public bodies to settle cases of sexual misconduct, racism, pregnancy discrimination, and other human rights violations.

The group now lobbies governments to recognise NDAs are currently being used to create dangerous environments.

In 2022 Glamour magazine wrote an article about NDA abuse and how the gagging of a victim or whistleblower comes at great psychological and sometimes physical cost to the signatory.[xcvi] The article states that 90% of the women who had signed an NDA had experienced a negative impact on their mental health, 'being silenced is choking,' preventing women from telling people what happened, often out of fear and potential financial ramifications.

Research by the campaign group *Pregnant Then Screwed* estimates close to half a million mothers have been silenced by NDAs.[xcvii] Mary O'Connor, formerly the UK Chief executive at KPMG has gone on record to say 'NDAs can be used to silence victims and enable perpetrators to misbehave.[xcviii] In Australia, a Reuters article stated Companies, BHP and RIO pressured women to sign NDAs after sexual harassment complaints. NDAs have become the default solution for organisations and public bodies to settle cases of sexual misconduct, racism, pregnancy discrimination, and other human rights violations.

However, NDAs don't protect the victim; they protect the employer's reputation and the career of the perpetrator. A study by Lizzie Barnes on *Silencing at Work, Sexual Harassment, Workplace Misconduct and NDAs*[xcix] led her to theorise the UK's superficially protective framework of individual employment and equality rights, while having emancipatory features, ultimately reinforces workplace hierarchy and often patriarchy.

These processes reinforce 'Organisational Silence', a term coined by Elizabeth Wolfe and Frances Milliken[c] where the upward flow of information is prevented out of fear, impeding an organisations growth. Regardless of its diverse mix of people, expressed views are silenced and so the organisation cannot benefit from its diversity.

Laura, a HR Business Partner shared her concerns with us: 'Like many organisations, the company I worked for sought to ramp our diversity hiring programme between 2015 and 2022. With the help of a newly formed employee resource group, our leadership crafted messaging to ensure women we hired felt they had a voice and could speak up if they saw patterns of discrimination or experienced it.'

She adds: 'The opposite happened. We silenced women instead of dealing with problem leaders. One leader achieved phenomenal results year-over-year but was horrific in his treatment of many women who worked for him, including having affairs with several assistants. He abused his power and was given free reign to do so, not just once, but twice in the same organisation. The women were exited and silenced and he was moved sideways for a period of time and then into another leadership position. Still, he retained his position, his salary, and his stock. He did not suffer; the women did.'

Laura also witnessed similar with women of colour speaking out about discriminatory behaviour they experienced in a new team that they joined. 'These women exited very quickly, one woman was brilliant at her role and 3 months after speaking out, she was gone with an NDA and settlement, she was heartbroken to leave and had a breakdown afterwards.'

Laura shares how employees are 'pressured' into accepting settlements: 'From the tone of official emails and the legal language used, it all creates anxiety. We would often put a timebound offer in place and state it would be rescinded after a certain time, to pressure an employee into taking a lower offer. It was all about protecting the organisation and dispensing with the individual as quickly as possible. In many cases, our employee had to seek additional legal support at their own cost.'

For a while, it seemed these concerns about NDA abuse in the workplace were being heard. The UK Parliament was actively addressing the misuse of NDAs in cases of workplace harassment and discrimination. The NDA Bill was introduced by MP Maria Millar, aiming to restrict the use of NDAs in concealing workplace misconduct. However, it did not advance into law.

In 2024, the UK Treasury Select Committee conducted an inquiry into 'Sexism in the City', after uncovering a shocking prevalence of sexism and misogyny in the UK's Financial Services industry, it called for a ban on NDAs in Financial Services. The UK Treasury acknowledged NDAs are used to 'intimidate victims of discrimination and harassment into silence.'

However, it failed to uphold an outright ban, arguing there is a legitimate place for NDAs to protect commercially sensitive information and Intellectual property - just not the people working for these companies, it seems.

The organisation committed to bring forward legislation outlining NDAs cannot be legally enforced if they prevent victims from reporting a crime.' As we write, another UK sector, the property industry, has launched a survey to understand the experience of women in residential property, sharing anecdotal evidence of women's voices being suppressed, 'including the use of NDAs to silence them.'[ci]

This growing need to evaluate these legal shackles begs the question: when will governments start to listen to women? Currently they are failing 50% of their population in more ways than one; A modern extension of historical structures aimed at controlling women's voices and maintain gender inequality.

The impact of workplace discrimination, NDA silencing, and being forced into leaving a workplace, career and financial security has psychological, physical and financial ramifications.

Andrea, a 45-year-old ex-Chief Technology Officer shared her experience following a grievance process: 'It was like a fire, ravaging and destroying everything in its path. Within months, I lost my career, my financial security and many so-called friendships. I couldn't tell close colleagues what was happening because I was gagged due to the NDA. I had to lie to my team.

'I ended up in a terrible place from a psychological perspective, on the brink of a breakdown. My self-esteem was in tatters, much of it torn to shreds through the process, where my professionalism and conduct had been called into question. I was terrified that if I inadvertently shared something online or to a friend, they would sue me.'

Andrea adds: 'The sad thing is, I didn't want to leave. I honestly wanted to help the leader and to help us grow as an organisation, but his response to me speaking up was to become defensive and question my ability, it became an untenable situation to stay in. I was forced out with 6 months' salary, removal of my stock, a 12 month anti-compete clause plus gagging order. I had to push my lawyer hard to negotiate more for me and that cost me an additional £2,000 in fees. I can't explain how horrible the whole process makes you feel as a human being.'

A year on and Andrea hasn't returned to a corporate environment. 'I feel a lot of shame that this happened to me, and struggle to articulate why I am looking for a role, especially as I was only there for 9 months. I am a cyber security leader, the anti-compete clause has made it almost impossible to find similar work. As a leader I feel a failure that I couldn't make impactful change to the business, I feel I let down my team.'

When asked about the financial implications, Andrea shares how she hasn't paid her mortgage in 6 months, in order to stretch out her settlement payout. 'I am not paying National Insurance or into a pension currently, it's harder to find a role at these levels, the tech industry is cutting back and so roles are far and few between.'

Farah comments, 'If we believe women can have it all, do it all and be it all, then breaking the silence on discrimination, abuse, bullying, harassment and NDA abuse is paramount.'

Sharing her own experiences, she states, 'Men rarely hear, you don't need to work you have a rich wife, nor are they discriminated against for having a family and choosing them over after-work drinks.'

Whilst she was initially scared to speak up for fear of losing her job, she emphasises, 'we need to allow women's voices to be heard, believed and upheld. I feel very strongly about this and am driven to change the harmful rhetoric in organisations.'

The stories and data presented in this chapter paint a picture of how NDAs and systemic discrimination continue to undermine women's agency and professional growth. The misuse of NDAs is not merely a legal mechanism, it is a tool of control that perpetuates inequality, shields perpetrators, and silences those who most need to be heard. This silencing does not only harm individual women but perpetuates cultures of secrecy and inequity that stifle progress for everyone.

Sam concludes: 'Organisations must stop using NDAs to protect their brand against misconduct and instead create cultures of transparency and accountability.'

Our observations are that many organisations have weak accountability structures - boards and leaders who fail to challenge executives, ineffective whistleblower protections and ethics policies that exist in name only. When investigations do occur, they are often internal and lack transparency, allowing organisations to control the narrative.

Governments must implement clear legislation that restricts the misuse of NDAs and empowers victims to speak without fear of reprisal. Leaders, too, must recognise the profound responsibility they hold in shaping workplace cultures and use their influence to dismantle harmful practices.

As Farah so aptly says: 'Enough is enough. This is not just about individual women's stories, it is about rewriting the narrative for all women, challenging systems of silence, and creating workplaces where every voice is valued, heard, and protected.'

The time for change is long overdue. Breaking the silence is not just a moral imperative, it is a societal one. Let this serve as a call to action for leaders, legislators, and organisations to end the gagging of women and instead champion their voices as the driving force for equality, justice, and progress.

#3 Shifting from Silence to Sisterhood

In The Mother of All Questions,[cii] Rebecca Solnit writes, 'Silence is what allows people to suffer without recourse… If our voices are essential to our humanity, to be rendered voiceless is to be dehumanised or excluded from one's humanity'. For centuries, systems of power have sought to divide and silence women, severing the natural bonds of togetherness and collaboration that could enable collective strength.

Research shows that women often adopt a 'tend-and-befriend'[ciii] approach to cope with challenges, nurturing connections and building networks of trust and understanding rather than adopting traditional 'fight or flight' behaviours. It's believed this behaviour evolved as a survival mechanism, particularly during times of danger, when forming alliances and protecting offspring would increase the likelihood of survival.

Central to this response is the role of oxytocin. Elevated levels of this hormone, particularly during stressful times are thought to drive women's instincts to seek support and build solidarity. In the modern world, this response manifests in women's inclination to create safe networks, spaces for sharing struggles and fostering understanding and offering and receiving compassion, we see this play out in women's communities, although our busy lives often lead us to neglect these ancient and important networks of sisterhood.

Interestingly, the power of storytelling increases oxytocin,[civ] helping women to bond and playing a crucial role in social connection, becoming a vehicle for healing, where community and connection become tools for emotional resilience, sisterhood and empowerment. Our nervous systems require this co-regulation and connection.

Sisterhood in professional spaces creates networks of safety, opportunity and story-sharing. Women supporting women, can amplify each other's voices, share experiences and address challenging topics that are often neglected in traditional corporate environments.

Female Staffers during President Obama's administration implemented sisterhood in the form of 'amplification', breaking the silence to ensure women's voices were heard in meetings. When a woman made a key point, other women would repeat it and give credit to its originator. This approach made the idea harder to ignore or appropriate, compelling acknowledgement from male colleagues. Over time this method contributed to increased female representation in senior roles within the administration.

Women's Employee Resource Groups can become drivers of cultural transformation in the workplace. Sam, reflecting on her tenure as chair of a women's community in a global tech firm, shares: 'when women connected at events, sharing their stories, the energy was electric. Conversations around menopause, racism, career building, and gender-based violence, were transformational for the culture of our company and for the empowerment of the women we hired. Importantly, they created an opportunity to break the silence for our male colleagues too and bring them into all important conversations and give them a chance to be heard. This was such a momentous breakthrough.'

Sam continues: 'Being vulnerable, being brave and telling stories was at the heart of this, what I've observed is when women speak up, it leads the way for men to follow too.' From experience, it's vital that senior leaders 'lean-in' and role model.'

Following an event in the US, Sam recalls how impactful running a programme of mentoring talks with senior women leaders was for the women attendees. 'We coached the female leaders to tell stories, be vulnerable, relatable, and to remove the corporate mask, this was such a game-changer in the sessions and the feedback was exceptional, with attendees sharing, "oh, so and so leader is just like me, perhaps I can become the next leader of this department."

It broke down so many barriers, brokered networks and relationships between the women. I also think it made the senior women feel more connected and less isolated too.'

Sam's point highlights an overlooked truth: sisterhood is about listening and learning across differences, generational, cultural, and experiential. It is in these spaces of trust and connection that women can share stories and begin to break the silence on the struggles they face and find solutions to fix them too, both at work and in the community.

Sam's journey led her to become a women's circle facilitator. 'I was fortunate to learn from several phenomenal women elders, across multiple indigenous communities. This was a life changing experience for me, for the very first time I was exposed to authentic, feminine and balanced leadership, women in harmony with themselves, each other, their land and people.

It was such a different way of being compared to the way women are forced to behave in corporate spaces, where women can emulate and embody very masculine principles to survive, yet these women I was learning from were incredibly powerful.'

Sadly, despite the innate potential that sisterhood holds for women, patriarchal structures keep us divided and often demonise sisterhood and community. However, historians do not believe it was always this way. Archaeologist and Anthropologist Marija Gimbutas (1921-1994), posits 'Old Europe' consisted of matrifocal societies, that revered the feminine through goddess worship, evidenced through the structures, artefacts and drawings available to us today.

Anne Baring, a prominent Jungian analyst and author argues how the transition to hierarchical, patriarchal systems marginalised women's collective power and silenced the feminine voice in social realms. [cv] Through her study of mythology, history and spirituality, she discusses the loss of the sacred feminine alongside the psychological impact of patriarchy.

Baring argues the suppression of feminine values (intuition, cooperation, emotional intelligence, and holistic wisdom) has led to a society obsessed with control, conquest and separation from nature. She calls for a need for balance, instead of rejecting masculinity, she advocates for the reintegration of the feminine principle to create a shift towards collaborative leadership, respect for intuition and valuing emotional intelligence as much as logic.

We don't share these stories in our academic institutions, a quick scour of the UK's History Key Stages Syllabus and it returns a fixation loaded toward war, colonialisation and the Industrial revolution. Everything is served in favour of the patriarchy. Sure, we make mention of British and Scottish Queen's and the suffragette movement, but rarely are women discussed in terms of our contribution to society, nor are contemporary perspectives offered that provide a different view on the role of women in religion.

We've had to fight to share the stories of women scientists who changed the world with their contributions. Feminine principles or the benefits of a matriarchal society are dismissed without discussion.

Many indigenous societies still uphold matrilineal descent and those that are male-led support egalitarian practices where women are revered for their spiritual leadership and serve as advisors or decision makers to ensure balance and respect in their communities. Māori women, particularly *Kuia* (elder women), hold respected positions in guiding family and community decisions. The women participate in sacred rituals as keepers of genealogical knowledge and many Māori women have been prominent leaders in movements to reclaim land and preserve cultural heritage.

The Mapuche women, called Machi, are the spiritual leaders and healers, custodians of medicinal knowledge and hold significant cultural authority of the Mapuche people of Chile and Argentina. In Ghana, the AKAN women hold significant political power, active in trade and economic activities, often leading markets and financial networks.

Haudenosaunee women, particularly clan mothers, hold significant political and social authority. Women are seen as givers of life and keepers of the land. In fact, early American feminists were heavily influenced by the Haudenosaunee women. The Haudenosaunee's egalitarian society served as a model for early feminists like Elizabeth Cady Stanton and Matilda Gage. Ticuna Women (South America) are often responsible for passing down oral histories, myths and traditional knowledge. The Kayapo women (Brazil), play a central role in preserving the rainforest, often acting as leaders, advocating for indigenous land rights.

Perhaps, the wisdom of indigenous women offers a powerful blueprint for reclaiming sisterhood and rediscovering our own lineage as women. Their reverence for connection, storytelling and collective leadership teaches us that the bonds between women are more than a source of strength, they are a foundation for a thriving world.

Breaking the silence to share our stories, celebrating our contributions and recognising the role of sisterhood in building our resilience and evolution is surely paramount for our journey in modern society. Paying attention to these narratives and seeking out these stories is not just an act of remembrance; it's a call to action. Inviting us to create spaces where women can be heard, to learn from each other and challenge the traditional male-centric narratives and biases that dominate our history today.

Breaking the silence through sisterhood becomes the foundation for future where every woman's voice is valued, respected and celebrated, sisterhood is allyship, a key component in the fight against discrimination.

#4 – Silenced by Numbers - Financial Literacy for Women, the road to Financial Empowerment

In chapter 3 we talked about financial health and gender pay and wealth gaps. In this section we want to break the silence on the financial literacy gender gap. Financial literacy is crucial for women's overall independence and well-being.

Financial literacy creates more than just economic security, it's a psychological and societal shift. According to *The Psychology of Money* by Morgan Housel and Dr Brad Klontz, our financial decisions are influenced by personal narratives and conditioning. Breaking free from these constraints requires women to reframe money as a tool for freedom and empowerment rather than a source of anxiety or shame.

Numerous memes and stereotypes about women and money depict us as frivolous spenders or poor financial planners. Social media trends like 'Girl Math', while seemingly innocuous, subtly reinforce the notion that we lack financial acumen and diminish our capabilities. Perhaps it's the old-fashioned notion that financial skills belong to left-brained people, often associated with masculine principles of logic, rationality and detachment.

Iain McGilchrist, in *The Master and His Emissary*, challenges this oversimplified left-brain/right-brain dichotomy, arguing instead that the left hemisphere, which focuses on categorisation, control and narrow focus, has historically been privileged in Western thought over the right hemisphere, which is more attuned to context, relationships and embodied understanding.

This bias has led to cultural overevaluation of quantifiable, 'rational' skills - often coded as masculine - while undervaluing intuitive, relational and holistic intelligence, traits more commonly associated with women. When financial decision making is framed purely in left-hemisphere terms, it reinforces a perception that women's ways of engaging with money, considering long-term security, ethical investment, and communal well-being, are less legitimate.

The stereotype of women as irrational spenders is not just outdated but deeply tied to a broader cultural bias that dismisses right-hemisphere strengths - intuition, emotional intelligence, and contextual reasoning - as secondary. Financial acumen is not about rigid logic alone, but about balancing analytical reasoning with relational insight and long-term vision, areas where many women excel but are rarely recognised.

Farah's story highlights the challenges women face, finding the time and energy to learn about investments, financial planning and setting time aside to plan. Her high-earning career, which appeared successful from the outside, left her with little capacity to navigate the complexities of financial management. Overwork and trying to juggle multiple priorities caused immense stress, leading to burnout.

This stark wakeup call forced her to reassess her priorities. She recalls thinking, 'I realised the futility of earning a substantial income without understanding how to manage it effectively.' From this pivotal moment, Farah prioritised her own financial education, uncovering a profound truth which she shares, 'True wealth is not just about earning money but knowing how to grow and protect it.'

Farah often reflects on the wisdom of her father who emphasised the importance of education and earning one's own income as the foundation of financial autonomy. His advice was a guiding principle in her life, shaping her belief that financial literacy is not only empowering but an essential life skill. It reinforced her commitment to helping other women embrace financial independence as a pathway to confidence and security.

Farah continues, 'We need to aggressively challenge the narratives and discrimination that forms around women and money. How many times have you heard that you're not good at saving money?' She concludes, 'This kind of comment angers me. Women often spend to their limit in terms of their contribution to the day-to-day running of the household from their income and this is putting them at a disadvantage, only to be accused of not being good with money!'

Several factors contribute to the financial literacy gap, including lower confidence levels among women. Yet according to the lifetime model created by Lusardi and Mitchell (2014) individuals who receive financial education outperform vs the those who don't.

Addressing the gap requires us to highlight it and talk about its impact in terms of women's wealth and target financial programmes tailored to women's unique need and circumstances. Women are more likely to experience career disruption over their lifetime, especially if they have children, their financial strategy needs to be different. There is a lot of evidence to suggest that such targeted programmes can significantly improve women's financial outcomes.

In their book, *Women Don't Ask: Negotiation and the Gender Divide*, Linda Babcock and Sara Leschever explain that women who negotiate their starting salary can yield an additional $1 million over their career. This highlights the financial gains women can unlock through education and assertiveness.

Financial literacy starts with honesty about our emotions and how we feel about money, wealth creation and our worth. If you're over 30 and reading this book, you may be feeling the hot flush of shame and guilt about your own financial knowledge. Stop. Instead of procrastinating - claiming that you will someday take control of your finances - reframe and say that this is day one of taking ownership for my financial future.

As Sam shares, 'I run women's circles on worth and every single woman who attends these circles feels guilty about asking for money. For those in salaried employment they feel guilty or shame when they ask for a pay increase to level them up. We have a real psychological block about wealth, value and worth.'

In his book, Dr Brad Klontz identifies 'money scripts' - unconscious beliefs about money developed in childhood. According to Klontz these scripts significantly influence financial behaviours and can lead to money disorders if not addressed.

The four scripts are:

Money Avoidance – People who avoid money, believe it's bad or corrupt and wealthy people are greedy. Individuals with this script believe they don't deserve money and tend to avoid financial matters.

Money Worship – People who worship money believe it will solve all problems and bring happiness. People with this script often have excessive focus on earning or accumulating wealth.

Money Status – People believe that self-worth is tied to net worth, Individuals with this script equate financial success to personal success and may seek to impress others through material possessions.

Money Vigilance – Individuals will save money and be financially cautious, often to the point of anxiety or excessive frugality.

While Klontz's approach emphasises personal behaviour, it underestimates the additional barriers women face. For example, the prevailing stereotypes, the fact that despite near equal access in the western world, women are less likely to use their accounts for savings; women score lower on financial literacy assessments than men, and the over-riding factor, it's been only 50 years since women were able to open a bank account without male co-signees.

Gen X women are the hardest hit by this. They grew up at a time where their own mothers received minimal to zero financial education.

The good news is that slowly change is happening. There is a growth in financial platforms aimed at women as well as a growing number of financial content creators and influencers, on Instagram and TikTok. *Ellevest* is a US based investment platform designed for women, *FemaleInvest* is a Danish company offering educational content and investment platforms for women and *Smartpurse* is a UK based financial wellness platform for women, offering financial literacy courses, budgeting tools and investment advice.

The path forward lies in a mix of neuroeconomics, community, education, accessible content, diverse role models, and content creators. Neuroeconomics - an interdisciplinary field combining neuroscience, psychology, and economics - offers valuable insights into how we make financial decisions. By understanding how their brains process risk, reward, and financial choices, women can gain powerful tools to improve financial literacy and confidence. This emerging field presents an exciting opportunity to reshape how women engage with money and financial independence.

Breaking the silence on women's financial literacy and empowerment is a crucial step towards equality.

We believe all schools and universities should offer financial literacy for all as a part of the curriculum. There is a significant emphasis placed on STEM subjects, but we need to go a step further to create financially literate people who can thrive in our chaotic economies.

#5 – Silence in Relationships - Evolving Communication to Enable Equality

Silence in relationships takes many forms - unspoken needs, suppressed emotions, withheld truths. It manifests in intimate relationships, friendships, workplaces and families shaping power dynamics in ways we rarely acknowledge but often feel. As we listened to women's stories and reviewed the written narratives in our survey, one theme became clear: communication is at the heart of equality, yet too often it is fractured, dismissed or weaponised.

Great communication isn't just about words exchanged; it's the entire emotional, physical and non-verbal dialogue that happens with every interaction. The micro-statements, the energy of a conversation, the tone shifts, the way someone looks away instead of responding.

When communication is strong, it fosters mutual respect, understanding, and safety. But when it falters, it leads to misalignment, resentment, and emotional disconnection. Many people, particularly in long-term relationships, feel unheard - leading to a sense of invisibility, a slow erosion of emotional safety that leaves them wondering: *Do I even matter?*

To feel safe in a relationship is to trust that you can express yourself without fear of judgment, retaliation, or dismissal. Emotional safety allows for vulnerability, for truth-telling, for deep intimacy. Many of the women shared they did not have this safety. Their concerns and feelings were invalidated, misinterpreted, or ignored. The men we spoke to felt the same way.

This same dynamic exists in the workplace. Employees who feel unheard, dismissed, or belittled eventually quiet-quit, disengage, or burn out. Communication doesn't begin with words; it begins with psychological safety - the ability to speak without fear.

Why do so many of us struggle to express ourselves? The answer lies in our nervous system

According to Dr. Stephen Porges' **Polyvagal Theory**, our nervous system determines how we engage with others based on whether we feel safe or threatened.

When we feel safe, we access the **ventral vagal state**, which allows for open, engaged, and thoughtful communication.

When we feel threatened, we shift into **fight-or-flight mode**, where we become defensive, reactive, or withdrawn.

When stress is overwhelming, we enter **dorsal vagal shutdown** - a state of numbness and detachment, where all communication stops. where we disconnect entirely, retreating into numbness.

This happens in relationships all the time. One person raises a concern, the other feels criticised and reacts defensively, and instead of listening, both talk at each other rather than with each other. Or worse - one person shuts down completely.

Many of us live in a state of chronic stress, rushing through conversations without considering how our nervous system - or our partner's - is influencing the exchange. The difference between a regulated and dysregulated conversation can determine whether a relationship deepens or deteriorates. The next time you feel a conversation becoming tense, ask yourself: *What does my nervous system need right now? How do I help my partner feel safe enough to listen?*

A common cause of communication breakdown is the "mind-reading fallacy" - the belief that others should intuitively understand our needs without us having to say them. This expectation leads to frustration when those needs go unmet.

Women are socially conditioned to minimise their feelings to avoid being seen as too dramatic, difficult, or demanding. Men are conditioned to suppress emotions, equating vulnerability with weakness. This creates a cycle: women feel unheard, men feel attacked, and both withdraw, leading to resentment and eventual shutdown.

To break this pattern, we must develop emotional literacy and emotional agility. Emotional literacy is the ability to recognise and name emotions in ourselves and others. Emotional agility is the ability to respond to emotions without being controlled by them. For men, this often means unlearning the idea that vulnerability is weakness. Being emotionally present and communicative is not a burden - it's a strength. For women, emotional literacy means voicing needs without guilt and recognising when they are internalising frustration rather than asserting their boundaries.

Too often, when a loved one is upset, we rush to "fix" the problem rather than simply listen. But not everything needs a solution -sometimes, people just need to be heard. A simple yet powerful practice is asking, "Do you want advice, or do you just want to vent?" This small shift can reduce conflict, deepen connection, and create space for honest dialogue.

Women often described feeling dismissed or ignored when expressing the same concern multiple times. Their efforts were reframed as "nagging" rather than legitimate communication. The word "nag" comes from Old Norse and Middle English roots meaning "to nibble" or "to pick at." By the 17th century, it had become a term used to silence women. But what is labelled as "nagging" is often simply a repeated attempt to be heard.

If we shift the perspective, the double standard becomes clear. In a workplace setting, follow up is seen as part of leadership - goals established, deadlines agreed, and accountability is expected. Yet in relationships, when women repeatedly seek resolution, it's dismissed as nagging.

Why is structured communication acceptable at work, but in a relationship, a woman expressing ongoing needs is seen as excessive? One of the most important shifts couples and workplaces can make is the development of emotional literacy and agility - the ability to recognise, understand, and appropriately respond to emotions in oneself and others.

Emotional literacy is more than just identifying feelings; it's about sitting with discomfort, validating emotions, and engaging constructively. It requires both self-awareness and the ability to meet others where they are.

However, literacy alone is not enough; emotional agility is what allows individuals to move through emotions without being controlled by them. Rather than acting impulsively, emotionally agile individuals acknowledge their feelings but choose their responses based on their values and long-term goals.

Shifting from witnessing to active listening is a transformative way to repair communication. When we create space for others to express themselves without fear of judgment, relationships deepen. True communication requires vulnerability, and vulnerability can be terrifying - especially for those who have been dismissed before. For women, speaking up often feels like a risk. For men, showing emotion can feel like an exposure of weakness. But it is in these spaces of mutual vulnerability that the strongest relationships are built.

Silence is never neutral - it is always used as a tool of control. Across history, women's voices have been erased, dismissed, or strategically silenced. The message has remained deafening amidst the silence: **Stay quiet, don't disrupt, don't demand too much.** But as history shows us, silence is never the final word. The act of breaking the silence, of shattering the myth, is more than just speaking up - it is an act of reclamation.

Reclaiming our space in history, in workplaces, in relationships, in financial systems, and in leadership means naming what has been deliberately obscured and calling out the structures that benefit from women's compliance. The pattern is clear: women are conditioned to soften their voices for others. But what if we stop accommodating? What if we leaned into radical honesty instead of shrinking into palatable diplomacy? Undoing the suppression of our voices must be an intentional act.

The question we must ask ourselves is this: What will we choose to remain silent about, and what will we refuse to let go unheard?

Silence never protected us. But breaking it? That is how we reclaim everything that was taken.

A Note to Male Allies

True allyship goes beyond awareness - it requires action. As you can see from this chapter, women's voices have been dismissed, controlled and erased for centuries, and that silencing continues today in subtler ways - being interrupted in meetings, dismissed as nagging, fired for speaking up against discrimination. In some countries the silencing prevents women from accessing an education. Women need allies to break their silence, call out sexism when you see it, use your voice to advocate for change, amplify women's contributions, give them space to speak, believe them when they raise issues of improper behaviour. Above all - help us to dismantle the systems that hold us all back.

Sometimes when men read about oppression, they can feel guilt and shame and that can feel hard to deal with. Talk to your colleagues about the topics in this chapter, create safe spaces for men to feel vulnerable. Change won't happen without you.

Pause and Reflect

Reflect on moments in your life where you've felt silenced or dismissed. What steps can you take to reclaim your voice and advocate for open, respectful communication in those spaces?

How can you foster emotional safety in your relationships whether at home, work, or in your community so that everyone feels heard and valued?

What narratives about your own power and worth have you internalised over time? How might sharing your story help dismantle these beliefs and inspire others to do the same?

'Diversity is being invited to the party; inclusion is being asked to dance'.
– Verna Myers

Chapter Nine
A Future Beyond the Myth

Rather than see this as an ending, we hope this marks the beginning of a new era, a future beyond the myth, a future worth fighting for.

One truth we have learnt on this journey, unravelling the myth is complex. We do not wish to stand in the way of women's aspiration, ambition or progress. Our mission is to highlight the barriers women face in achieving their goals and lead the change this world desperately needs.

What is clear: It is the 'doing it all and being it all' that makes the 'having it all' unattainable for many women. Collectively, the cost of the myth is immense. Women burnout, shouldering the so-called invisible burdens that sustain families, communities, governments and corporations, and when women fall, so does society. Is this what we want for our women, for our daughters, our sisters and our friends? We must also acknowledge the impact on our men too. We think they deserve a better future as well.

The promise of gender equality remains just that, a **promise,** a north star, a paragraph in an annual report, a mission statement on a company wall. We have had enough of this near-constant denial of our human rights. We are the ones who birth nations, build economies and power societies, yet those same systems refuse to afford our basic rights, adequate maternity policies, recognition of the changes our bodies undergo, or the value of the work we do inside and outside our homes.

The world is facing many existential threats, **gender inequality must not be one of them. The anti-diversity movement must be halted.** Are we really telling our daughters they do not matter? Are we happy pushing harmful stereotypes onto our sons?

Our Manifesto for Change

Reinvent Education
Educational reform is essential. The obsessive focus on hyper achievement and academic grades must not come at the cost of psychological resilience, emotional intelligence and real-world skills. We need an education system that goes beyond producing test scores and instead nurtures self-awareness, confidence and autonomy in young women (and men).

From an early age, girls are conditioned to please, to prioritise being liked over being heard. They are praised for their politeness, their neat handwriting, their ability to sit still, while boys are encouraged to take risks, speak up and lead whilst deprioritising their emotional needs.

This conditioning follows them into adulthood. It shapes how they navigate relationships and careers. It's time to break the cycle.

Education must teach girls to trust their own judgement, not defer to legacy gender norms that dictate what they cannot or cannot do. Schools must remove the artificial divide between boy and girl activities. Girls need equal access to sports, leadership roles, hands on learning, and decision-making opportunities. Likewise, boys must have access to activities that support their emotional learning, communication skills and a holistic understanding of relationship and responsibility.

No subject, no ambition, no space, should feel off-limits.

We need self-defence classes taught in school as part of the physical education curriculum. Girls need access to debate clubs and public speaking to help them develop confidence in using their voices to advocate for themselves and others. We need a culture in schools that teaches girls they belong anywhere they choose to be, so that in the future they can create spaces they feel safe to occupy.

Beyond confidence, education must equip young women with financial literacy and autonomy. Too often, women enter adulthood without a clear understanding of investments, salary negotiations or wealth creation or how to build their own business. They are left to figure it out, decades later, often at a cost. Financial independence is not a luxury; it is a necessity, and it must be taught from an early age.

Girls need to grow up knowing their worth from their skills, intelligence and their ability to shape the world. Their value is not tied to beauty, nor should their aspirations be limited by silent social expectations. For a truly equitable future we must equip boys with the tools to engage in meaningful relationships, value collaboration and redefine strength beyond dominance or suppression of emotion.

A reformed education system is one that raises girls to be powerful not perfect, girls who seek power with, not power over. Girls who understand the need for harmony with this world, the need for respect, kindness and the power of communication versus war, coupled with the ability to use their voice without fear.

This reformed education system is one that raises boys to accept and respect vulnerability. One that teaches boys about consent and accountability, to be equals, not just bystanders. Boys who understand the need for emotional expression and regulation to help create harmony in this world, the need for respect, empathy and the power of collaboration.

It would teach our children to take risks, not just tests. A system that ensures when they do step into adulthood, they do so with confidence, capability and control over their futures.

Reshape policies

The Universal Declaration of Human Rights (Article 25) 'Right to Family Life & Wellbeing' states motherhood and childhood should be entitled to special care and assistance. Yet, in 2025, global maternity rights remain inconsistent, inadequate and inhumane in some of the world's wealthiest nations. The United States still has no federally mandated paid maternity leave, forcing millions of women to choose between financial stability and their own health and recovery. **This is not progress this is systemic neglect and abandonment.**

We need a globally mandated, universal maternity law to protect the rights of mothers and children. All working women must have access to 12 months of fully paid maternity leave, without penalty, career setbacks or financial insecurity. This must be a living wage equal to their salary, not a fraction, ensuring that women are not pushed out of the workforce for simply becoming mothers.

Anything less is a violation of fundamental human rights.

We also call for paternity leave to be increased to a minimum of 6 weeks. Father's have a fundamental right to support their families, beyond the traditional 'provider role'. Today, global paternity leave averages around 1-2 weeks. Enhanced paternity leave would help to shift traditional gender roles.

Shared parental leave must be fully paid and actively encouraged, ensuring that caregiving is no longer seen as women's work, but as a shared responsibility. Men taking parental and paternity leave is shown to reduce postpartum depression, increase female work participation and lead to a more equal division of household labour. The resistance to this change is cultural, not logistical and it must end.

More men must be encouraged to take their parental leave, we advocate for the model they have in Sweden, which mandates a non-transferrable, use it or lose it paternity leave to encourage fathers to take equal responsibility and organisations to support them.

We also ask for parental leave to be available for non-birthing and same-sex couples.

We call for a shift in thinking to view childcare as part of the social infrastructure of our society, as necessary as utilities, transportation and healthcare. Governments must provide affordable childcare, in partnership with employers. Childcare should be seen as an investment into the future economic stability of an equitable nation, not a cost to be cut.

In the UK, where childcare costs are among the highest in the world the government offers 30 hours of state-funded childcare per week for eligible families and from September 2025, this will be available for babies aged 9 months up. This leaves a critical gap for mothers who cannot afford to take extended leave or may be self-employed and are forced back to work before affordable childcare is available. If governments are serious about supporting women in the workforce, then state-funded childcare must start from 6 weeks post-partum.

Work contracts must be flexible by default.
It should not be a privilege; it is a necessity to all working parents. Women remain penalised for choosing part-time or flexible work. Governments must introduce stronger legal protections against discrimination for parents. We call for mandatory leadership development and career returner programmes. post leave for both men and women to support their return to work after a leave of absence.

Beyond motherhood, women's health across all life stages is still being dismissed. Menopause is not a private struggle; it is a workplace and societal issue. But still in the UK, access to menopause support is fragmented and inconsistent.

Routine hormone blood tests must become standard practise, no woman should have to fight for basic healthcare. Menopause treatments must be fully covered under health insurance, without additional fees and Hormone Replacement Therapy (HRT) must be free and accessible to all women globally. Women are not choosing to go through the menopause, nevertheless we are expected to bear the physical, emotional and financial consequences alone.

For too long the working world has refused to accommodate the realities of women's lives, from maternity to childcare to menopause to eldercare. It is not enough to have policies on paper if workplaces continue to punish women for using them.

Women should not have to beg for remote work, reduced hours or career continuity after maternity leave. We should not have to shout against discrimination that is happening in plain sight. We should not have to justify our need for a workplace that works with us, not against us.

The system is broken, not by accident, but by design. It was built this way, without women in mind and now it must be rebuilt with us, so we can thrive equally.

Transparent Gender & Discrimination reporting
Mandatory transparent reporting on leadership diversity, the gender pay, health and wealth gaps. Companies must be required to report on and uphold their diversity goals, ensuring real progress rather than performative compliance.

Additionally, we call for clear and public reporting on gender-based discrimination grievances within organisations. The widespread use of NDAs to silence women in discrimination cases must end.

No organisation should be able to hide its failings behind loopholes, we include government reporting in this mandate. Secrecy protects perpetrators it does not support progress.

Campaign for equality in the home

It is evident from the stories we have shared, and research conducted we need an urgent change to the narrative around invisible labour. We must redefine how society values care work. Childcare, eldercare and domestic labour - must be recognised, valued and shared. Governments must take an active role in shifting the narrative that communicates caregiving and household management as only women's responsibility to establishing it as a shared duty.

This is not just a cultural shift; it requires real policy change and accountability to ensure progress is more than just rhetoric and a campaign slogan. We need men to step up, not as helpers or bystanders, but as equal partners in both home and family life, equally women must let them. The cycle of over-responsibility and perfectionism that many women carry must be broken, because it is killing us. Equality at home is not about women delegating tasks; it is about redefining responsibility altogether.

Reimagining Economic Reform

The global economy remains shackled by structures that prioritise profit over people, infinite growth over wellbeing and competition over care. The world is changing, and it is time our economic thinking catches up. Traditional economic policies are built on a very outdated assumption of male-dominated workforces and female domestic labour.

The unpaid and underpaid labour of women - childcare, elder care, household management - underpins the very fabric of society yet remain systematically devalued and excluded from GDP calculations, dismissed as not real work. A balanced economic model would shift this paradigm, centering human well-being, gender equity and collective prosperity as real markers of success. It would recognise care work as the backbone of economic productivity rather than an invisible burden borne only by women.

A balanced economy is not about gender - it's about shifting from rigid, hierarchical, exploitative structures to a regenerative, inclusive and people-centred model of economic value.

Imagine an economy where care work is valued, financially compensated, included in GDP calculations or offset through universal care policies. Where success of a nation is measured by quality of life, equality indicators and social capital - not just GDP and stock markets. Where flexibility and time affluence replace burnout-driven productivity. The economy cannot function without care - yet we refuse to value it - that needs to change. Anything less is a betrayal to current and future generations.

Our new beginning isn't just about shattering a myth and this manifesto is not just about fairness - it's about breaking a cycle. The idea that women must 'do it all and be it all to have it all' has trapped generations in a system never designed for them, forcing them to juggle ambition, autonomy, and invisible labour, make sacrifices, while battling bias and burnout. Incremental progress and performative policies are not enough, gender equality cannot continue to be a distant promise or a corporate slogan - it must become our reality.

Women should not be expected to fit into a system that refuses to make space for them.

The system needs to be rebuilt with us, for all of us - so together we can create a future of collective prosperity, shared responsibility and real change, where balance, equity and opportunity are not luxuries, but inherent rights.

Together, we rise.
Together, we build.
Together, we create a future beyond the myth.

Acknowledgments

Writing this book has been a journey shaped by our personal experiences as mothers, professionals, and women navigating the complex demands of modern life. Balancing our careers with the responsibilities of family has been both rewarding and challenging, and this book reflects those struggles, triumphs, and lessons learned.

To our mothers, whose love, kindness, wisdom, and resilience shaped us into the women we are today, we are forever grateful. Your strength continues to guide and inspire us every step of the way.

To our daughters, you have been our greatest inspiration. We hope this book serves as a guide and a source of strength for you, as well as for all the women who come after us. May you grow up in a world where you are free to define your own success, free from the constraints and myths that held us back.

We also want to acknowledge the countless women who have shared their stories with us, whose experiences shaped this work, and whose courage in speaking out fuels the movement for change.

Finally, we extend our gratitude to everyone who supported us along the way, friends, family, and colleagues. Your encouragement helped bring this vision to life.

Bibliography

Alzheimer's Association. (2024). https://www.alz.org/

American Psychological Association. (2024). https://www.apa.org/

American Psychological Association. (2020). Stress in America, A National Mental Health Crisis

Jess Alberts & Sarah Tracy January 2011; An Integrative Theory of the Division of Domestic Labour: Threshold level, social organizing and sensemaking, Journal of family communications

Boston Consulting Group (BCG). (2019). Frances Brooks Taplett, Matt Krentz, Justin

BMJ. (2021). Women's Wellbeing and the Burden of Unpaid Work.

Catalyst. (2022). Women in Management (Quick Take).

Catalyst. (2023). Women in Male-Dominated Industries and Occupations (Quick Take).

Catherine Rottenberg. (2014). Feminist Studies. Happiness and the Liberal Imagination: How Superwoman Became Balanced.

Dan Butler. (2017). The Blue Zones of Happiness: Lessons from the World's Happiest People.

Dean, and Gabrielle Novacek. (2019). Diversity is Just the First Step, Inclusion Comes Next.

Caroline Criado Perez, Caroline Criado-Perez, et al. (2019). Invisible Women: Exposing Data Bias in a World Designed for Men.

Deloitte. (2023). Women at Work: A Global Outlook.

Deloitte. (2024). Gen Z and Millennial Survey.

Eve Rodsky (2021) Fair Play; Quercus

Forbes. Dr Ewelina U. Ochab. (November 2023) Violence Against Women and Girls Today: One Killed Every 11 Minutes.
https://www.forbes.com/sites/ewelinaochab/2023/11/25/violence-against-women-and-girls-today-one-killed-every-11-minutes/?sh=26a616f81e5d

GALLUP. (2023). State of the Global Workplace 2023 Report, The Voice of the World's Employees.

Gemma Hartley. (2018). Fed up; Emotional Labor, Women, and the Way Forward

Helen Gurley Brown. (1983). Having it All.

Hector Garcia, Francesc Miralles, Naoko Mori. (2017). Ikigai: The Japanese Secret to a Long and Happy Life.

Arlie Hochschild (1989, 2003, 2012). The Second Shift: Working Families and the Revolution at Home

Institute For Divorce Financial Analysts. Survey: Certified Divorce Financial Analyst® (CDFA®) professionals Reveal the Leading Causes of Divorce.

Jennifer Breheny Wallace. (2023). Never Enough.

Julianne Holt-Lunstad, PhD. (2018). The Potential Public Health Relevance of Social Isolation and Loneliness: Prevalence, Epidemiology, and Risk Factors.

KFF. (Mars 2021). Women, Work, and Family During COVID-19: Findings from the KFF Women's Health Survey.
https://www.kff.org/mental-health/issue-brief/women-work-and-family-during-covid-19-findings-from-the-kff-womens-health-survey/

Kim Kiyosaki. (April 2006). Rich Women: A Book on Investing for Women.

Iain McGilchrist (2010) The Master and his Emissary, Yale UP

McKinsey & Company. (2020). Diversity Wins: How Inclusion Matters Report.

McKinsey & Company and LeanIn.Org. (October 5, 2023). Women in the Workplace 2023 Report.

McKinsey & Company and LeanIn.Org. Women in the Workplace 2024 - 10th Anniversary Report.

McKinsey & Company. (2019). One is the Loneliest Number.

National Coalition Against Domestic Violence. (2020). Domestic Violence.

National Library of Medicine. (2010). Coronary heart disease in women: a challenge for the 21st century.
https://pubmed.ncbi.nlm.nih.gov/20126352/

Office for National Statistics. (May 2024). Families and Households in the UK: 2023

Office for National Statistics. (November 2023). Domestic Abuse in England and Wales Overview: November 2023.

Pew Research Center. (2015). Women more than men adjust their careers for family life.

https://www.pewresearch.org/short-reads/2015/10/01/women-more-than-men-adjust-their-careers-for-family-life/

Pew Research Center. (2013). Modern Parenthood.
https://www.pewresearch.org/social-trends/2013/03/14/modern-parenthood-roles-of-moms-and-dads-converge-as-they-balance-work-and-family/

Richard Fry. (August 2023). Almost 1 in 5 stay-at-home parents in the U.S. are dads.

Ruth Gaunt. Maternal Gatekeeping: Antecedents & Consequences, 2007, journal of family issues

Sheryl Sandberg. (2013). Lean In.

Shelter. (December 2023). Homelessness in England 2023.

SleepFoundation.org. (2013). Understanding Sleep Deprivation and New Parenthood. https://www.sleepfoundation.org/sleep-deprivation/parents

Sleep Research Society (SRS). (2019). Long-term effects of pregnancy and childbirth on sleep satisfaction and duration of first-time and experienced mothers and fathers.
https://academic.oup.com/sleep/article/42/4/zsz015/5289255

Statista. (2019). Women Work More Than Men.
https://www.statista.com/chart/13940/women-work-more-than-men/

Stanford University. (2015). Women leaders: Does likeability really matter?
https://gender.stanford.edu/news/women-leaders-does-likeability-really-matter

St Catherine University. (2022). Emotional in the Workplace: The Disproportionate Burden on Women.
https://www.stkate.edu/academics/women-in-leadership-degrees/empowering-women/emotional-labor-in-the-workplace

S&P Global. (October 2018). The Key to Unlocking U.S. GDP Growth: Women.

Sylvia Ann Hewlett. (March 2002). Creating a life: Professional Women and the Quest for Children.

Sweden.se (2024). https://sweden.se/work-business/working-in-sweden/work-life-balance

TalentLMS and SHRM. (2022). Research: The State of L&D in 2022, How training and development shape employee experience and empower organisational growth.
https://www.talentlms.com/employee-learning-and-development-stats

The BMJ. (August 2021). Women's wellbeing and the burden of unpaid work. https://www.bmj.com/content/374/bmj.n1972

The World Bank Data. (2024). https://data.worldbank.org

United Nations - Department of Economic and Social Affairs. (2024). https://www.un.org/en/desa

U.S. Bureau of Labor Statistics. (July 2022). How parents used their time in 2021. https://www.bls.gov/opub/ted/2022/how-parents-used-their-time-in-2021.htm

U.S. Bureau of Labor Statistics. (March 2022). Women in the labor force: a databook.

U.S. Bureau of Labor Statistics. (December 2015). Labor force projections to 2024: the labor force is growing, but slowly.

Wendy Patton. (January 2013). Conceptualising Women's Working lives – Volume 5.

Women's Aid Federation of Northern Ireland, Scottish Women's Aid and Welsh Women's Aid. (2023). The Annual Audit, The Domestic Abuse Report.

Woman's Budget Group. (November 2022). A green and caring economy.

World Economic Forum. (June 2023) Global Gender Gap Report 2023

World Economic Forum. (August 2023) Explainer: What are pay transparency laws and are they working?

Endnotes

[i] https://en.wikipedia.org/wiki/Resignation_of_Jacinda_Ardern
[ii] https://www.nytimes.com/2015/01/04/magazine/the-complicated-origins-of-having-it-all.html
[iii] https://www.nytimes.com/2015/01/04/magazine/the-complicated-origins-of-having-it-all.html
[iv] https://ftsewomenleaders.com/
[v] https://www.ft.com/content/a586a0d6-d299-463c-a531-22539446ff87
[vi] https://www.theguardian.com/business/2023/nov/05/over-the-glass-cliff-female-chief-executives-have-shorter-tenure-than-men-due-to-crisis-management-roles
[vii] https://www.ft.com/content/17606f25-1d03-4f37-b7f4-f39989af9bde?
[viii] https://aom.org/about-aom/aom-news/blog-detail_releases/blog-detail/news/2022/06/07/the-ladders-how-women-can-say-no-to-office-housework
[ix] Heavier Lies her Crown: Gendered Patterns of Leader Emotional Labor and their downstream effects; Andrea C Vial; Colleen M Cowgill; Front Psychol 2022 Vol 13
[x] 024 study by USC's Public Exchange and Center for the Changing Family
[xi] https://www.mckinsey.com/featured-insights/diversity-and-inclusion/women-in-the-workplace
[xii] https://www.progressive-policy.net/publications/what-women-want#:~:text=The%20think%20tank%27s%20latest%20report%2C%20What%20Women%20Want%2C,spending%20more%20time%20caring%20for%20adults%20than%20men.
[xiii] Reich-Stiebert, N., Froehlich, L. & Voltmer, JB. Gendered Mental Labor: A Systematic Literature Review on the Cognitive Dimension of Unpaid Work Within the Household and Childcare. *Sex Roles* **88**, 475–494 (2023). https://doi.org/10.1007/s11199-023-01362-0
[xiv] https://natcen.ac.uk/events/british-social-attitudes-2023
[xv] https://www.bls.gov/opub/ted/2022/how-parents-used-their-time-in-2021.htm
[xvi] Pew Research Center. (2013). Modern Parenthood. https://www.pewresearch.org/social-trends/2013/03/14/modern-parenthood-roles-of-moms-and-dads-converge-as-they-balance-work-and-family/
[xvii] Office for National Statistics. (May 2024). Families and households in the UK: 2023
[xviii] https://www.census.gov/newsroom/stories/single-parent-day.html
[xix] https://www.bbc.com/worklife/article/20210518-the-hidden-load-how-thinking-of-everything-holds-mums-back

[xx] https://www.unwomen.org/sites/default/files/2024-11/femicides-in-2023-global-estimates-of-intimate-partner-family-member-femicides-en.pdf
[xxi] Alberts, Jess & Tracy, Sarah & Trethewey, Angela. (2011). An Integrative Theory of the Division of Domestic Labor: Threshold Level, Social Organizing and Sensemaking. Journal of Family Communication. 11. 21-38. 10.1080/15267431.2011.534334.
[xxii] https://www.pewresearch.org/short-reads/2021/01/25/for-american-couples-gender-gaps-in-sharing-household-responsibilities-persist-amid-pandemic
[xxiii] https://www.huffingtonpost.co.uk/entry/weaponized-incompetence-women_l_61e71983e4b0d8b665717814
[xxiv] Brene Brown on partnerships https://www.youtube.com/watch?v=-l-ngh3qPZs
[xxv] https://www.weforum.org/agenda/2020/12/covid-women-workload-domestic-caring/
[xxvi] https://www.ons.gov.uk/peoplepopulationandcommunity/healthandsocialcare/healthandlifeexpectancies/bulletins/ukhealthindicators/2019to2020
[xxvii] https://www.sciencedaily.com/releases/2014/08/140819082912.htm
[xxviii] https://www.caregiver.org/resource/caregiver-health/
[xxix] Gaunt, R. (2008). Maternal Gatekeeping: Antecedents and Consequences. *Journal of Family Issues, 29*(3), 373-395. https://doi.org/10.1177/0192513X07307851
[xxx] Alberts, Jess K. , Tracy, Sarah J. and Trethewey, Angela(2011) 'An Integrative Theory of the Division of Domestic Labor: Threshold Level, Social Organizing and Sensemaking', Journal of Family Communication, 11: 1, 21 — 38
[xxxi] Eagly AH, Karau SJ. Role congruity theory of prejudice toward female leaders. Psychol Rev. 2002 Jul;109(3):573-98. doi: 10.1037/0033-295x.109.3.573. PMID: 12088246.
[xxxii] Jamieson, Kathleen Hall, Beyond The Double Bind: Women and Leadership (New York, NY, 1995; online edn, Oxford Academic, 31 Oct. 2023), https://doi.org/10.1093/oso/9780195089400.001.0001, accessed 27 Feb. 2025.
[xxxiii] https://textio.com/feedback-bias-2024
[xxxiv] Derks, B., van Laar, C., & Ellemers, N. (2016). The Queen Bee Phenomenon: Why Women Leaders Distance Themselves from Junior Women. The Leadership Quarterly, 27(3), 456–469. DOI:
[xxxv] Impression Management Theory; Erving Goffman, 1959
[xxxvi] Ryan, M. K., & Haslam, S. A. (2007). The Glass Cliff: Exploring the Dynamics Surrounding the Appointment of Women to Precarious Leadership Positions. *The Academy of Management Review, 32*(2), 549–572. http://www.jstor.org/stable/20159315
[xxxvii] https://www.deloitte.com/global/en/issues/work/content/genz-millennialsurvey.html

[xxxviii] https://welldoing.org/article/millennials-gen-z-understanding-your-relationship-work-burnout

[xxxix] https://dilanconsulting.com/managing-generation-x-in-the-workplace-through-a-dei-lens/

[xl] https://www.pewresearch.org/short-reads/2019/07/24/baby-boomers-us-labor-force/

[xlii] https://www.psychologytoday.com/us/basics/burnout#Burnout_Definition

[xliii] https://info.mavenclinic.com/pdf/parents-at-the-best-workplaces?submissionGuid=5ac95855-8079-46ac-9ba5-f8b11c2ae5c5

[xliv] Wang, S., Li, L. Double Jeopardy: The Roles of Job Autonomy and Spousal Gender Ideology in Employed Women's Mental Health. *Applied Research Quality Life* **18**, 473–490 (2023). https://doi.org/10.1007/s11482-022-10090-8

[xlv] https://www.thelancet.com/journals/lanpub/article/PIIS2468-2667(22)00160-8/fulltext

[xlvi] https://www.bmj.com/content/374/bmj.n1972

[xlvii] Stall NM, Shah NR, Bhushan D. Unpaid Family Caregiving—The Next Frontier of Gender Equity in a Postpandemic Future. *JAMA Health Forum.* 2023;4(6):e231310. doi:10.1001/jamahealthforum.2023.1310

[xlviii] Kim GH, Lee HS, Jung SW, Lee JG, Lee JH, Lee KJ, Kim JJ. Emotional labor, workplace violence, and depressive symptoms in female Bank employees: a questionnaire survey using the K-ELS and K-WVS. Ann Occup Environ Med. 2018 Mar 12;30:17. doi: 10.1186/s40557-018-0229-9. PMID: 29564140; PMCID: PMC5848577.

[xlix] Aung N, Tewogbola P. The impact of emotional labor on the health in the workplace: a narrative review of literature from 2013-2018. AIMS Public Health. 2019 Aug 20;6(3):268-275. doi: 10.3934/publichealth.2019.3.268. PMID: 31637276; PMCID: PMC6779598.

[l] Stuenkel, C. A. (2024). Cardiovascular disease in women: take it to heart. *Climacteric*, 27(1), 2–4. https://doi.org/10.1080/13697137.2023.

[li] https://www.health.harvard.edu/blog/sleep-well-and-reduce-your-risk-of-dementia-and-death-2021050322508

[lii] https://www.ifm.org/news-insights/understanding-psychoemotional-roots-immune-disease/

[liii] https://www.mckinsey.com/mhi/our-insights/closing-the-womens-health-gap-a-1-trillion-dollar-opportunity-to-improve-lives-and-economies

[liv] https://www.bls.gov/opub/mlr/2015/article/labor-force-projections-to-2024.htm

[lv] https://www.moodysanalytics.com/-/media/article/2023/Close-the-Gender-Gap-to-Unlock-Productivity-Gains.pdf

[lvi] https://www.weforum.org/stories/2024/03/women-startups-vc-funding/

[lvii] https://cles.org.uk/wp-content/uploads/2024/03/Womens-Work.pdf
[lviii] https://institutedfa.com/cdfa-professionals-reveal-leading-causes-of-divorce
[lix] Gender Differences in Saving and Investing Behaviours; Xuewei Qiao; 2012
[lx] Ran Gu, Cameron Peng, Weilong Zhang, The Gender Gap in Household Bargaining Power: A Revealed-Preference Approach, The Review of Financial Studies, 2024;, hhae039, https://doi.org/10.1093/rfs/hhae039
[lxi] https://www.youngwomenstrust.org/our-research/young-women-and-economic-abuse

[lxiii] https://www.weforum.org/publications/global-gender-gap-report-2023/
[lxiv] https://www.weforum.org/agenda/2023/08/gender-pay-gap-salary-transparency/
[lxv] https://www.thirdway.org/report/the-fatherhood-bonus-and-the-motherhood-penalty-parenthood-and-the-gender-gap-in-pay
[lxvi] https://read.dukeupress.edu/demography/article/58/1/247/167586/Motherhood-Penalties-and-Fatherhood-Premiums
[lxvii] https://www.weforum.org/agenda/2022/07/women-wealth-equity-index-gender-gap/
[lxviii] https://www.wbg.org.uk/publication/spirals-of-inequality/
[lxix] https://www.wbg.org.uk/collection/commission-on-a-gender-equal-economy/
[lxx] https://www.wtwco.com/en-gb/insights/2022/11/europe-global-gender-wealth-equity-index
[lxxi] https://www.caregiver.org/resource/caregiver-statistics-work-and-caregiving
[lxxii] https://www.ted.com/talks/brene_brown_listening_to_shame?subtitle=en
[lxxiii] Luck T, Luck-Sikorski C. The wide variety of reasons for feeling guilty in adults: findings from a large cross-sectional web-based survey. BMC Psychol. 2022 Aug 12;10(1):198. doi: 10.1186/s40359-022-00908-3. PMID: 35962455; PMCID: PMC9373443.
[lxxiv] Curran, T., & Hill, A. P. (2019). Perfectionism is increasing over time: A meta-analysis of birth cohort differences from 1989 to 2016. Psychological Bulletin, 145(4), 410–429. https://doi.org/10.1037/bul0000138
[lxxv] https://www.forbes.com/sites/kimelsesser/2021/10/05/heres-how-instagram-harms-young-women-according-to-research/
[lxxvi] https://muse.jhu.edu/article/829152
[lxxvii] https://www.bbc.com/worklife/article/20210712-paternity-leave-the-hidden-barriers-keeping-men-at-work
[lxxviii] https://www.theguardian.com/lifeandstyle/2022/jan/27/women-child-free-30-ons
[lxxix] https://maternityaction.org.uk/a-perfect-storm/

[lxxxi] https://www.theatlantic.com/magazine/archive/2012/07/why-women-still-cant-have-it-all/309020/

[lxxxii] https://www.local.gov.uk/our-support/workforce-and-hr-support/wellbeing/menopause/menopause-factfile

[lxxxiii] https://www.cipd.org/uk/knowledge/guides/menopause-people-professionals-guidance/

[lxxxiv] https://www.healtheuropa.com/menopausal-women-suicide-rates-are-at-their-highest-since-1996/111752/

[lxxxv] https://www.equalityhumanrights.com/guidance/menopause-workplace-guidance-employers?return-url=https%3A%2F%2Fwww.equalityhumanrights.com%2Fsearch%3Fkeys%3Dmenopause

[lxxxvi] https://www.theguardian.com/society/2021/aug/17/my-bosses-were-happy-to-destroy-me-the-women-forced-out-of-work-by-menopause

[lxxxvii] https://www.britsafe.org/safety-management/2022/menopause-at-work-women-need-better-support-from-employers

[lxxxviii] https://www.nhmenopausesociety.org/menopause-puts-final-nail-in-marriage-coffin/

[lxxxix] https://www.newsonhealth.co.uk/

[xc] https://www.maturitas.org/article/S0378-5122(16)30284-5/abstract

[xci] https://www.fastcompany.com/90863592/women-leadership-feel-lonely-isolated

[xcii] https://paminy.com/book-summary-of-boys-and-men/

[xciii] Kim ES, Shiba K, Boehm JK, Kubzansky LD. Sense of purpose in life and five health behaviors in older adults. Prev Med. 2020 Oct;139:106172. doi: 10.1016/j.ypmed.2020.106172. Epub 2020 Jun 25. PMID: 32593729; PMCID: PMC7494628.

[xciv] Caliban and the Witch: Women, the Body and Primitive Accumulation, 2004, Autonomedia, Silvia Federici

[xcv] https://www.pewresearch.org/short-reads/2017/12/14/gender-discrimination-comes-in-many-forms-for-todays-working-women/

[xcvi] https://www.glamourmagazine.co.uk/article/non-disclosure-agreement-abuse

[xcvii] https://www.goodto.com/family/family-news/nearly-half-a-million-mothers-legally-gagged-from-talking-about-wrokplace-discrimination-and-bulliyng-heres-how-you-can-help

[xcviii] https://www.fnlondon.com/articles/ex-kpmg-boss-ndas-can-be-used-to-silence-victims-and-enable-perpetrators-to-misbehave-e5b7b462

[xcix] Lizzie Barmes, Silencing at Work: Sexual Harassment, Workplace Misconduct and NDAs, *Industrial Law Journal*, Volume 52, Issue 1, March 2023, Pages 68–106, https://doi.org/10.1093/indlaw/dwac007

[c] Organizational Silence: A barrier to change and development in a pluralistic world, Wolfe, Milliken, NYU, Academy of management review, 2000, Vol. 25, No.4 706-723

[ci] https://womeninresidentialproperty.co.uk/survey2024/

[cii] The Mother of all Questions, Rebecca Solnit, 2017, Haymarket
[ciii] Shelley Taylor et al, 2000
[civ] https://www.psychologytoday.com/ca/blog/the-stories-of-our-lives/202106/storytelling-is-good-for-us-and-our-bodies
[cv] Anne Baring, The Dream of the Cosmos; A quest for the soul, 2019, Archive